past present  & future craft practice

Edited by
Louise Valentine
Georgina Follett

Published in 2010 by
NMS Enterprises Ltd – Publishing
National Museums Scotland
on behalf of University of Dundee

ISBN 978-1-905267-50-7

British Library Cataloguing in Publication Data
A catalogue record of this book is available from the British Library.

Design and Layout
Not Just Design

Printed in Great Britain by Butler Tanner & Dennis, Frome, Somerset

For a full listing of related NMS titles please visit:
www.nms.ac.uk/books

For further information concerning 'Past, Present and Future Craft Practice' please visit:
www.futurecraft.dundee.ac.uk
www.djcad.dundee.ac.uk

Contents

In some ways you can think of this book as an introduction to craft research – a new form of craft practice – with an alternative approach to developing craft and its economy in the twenty-first century. It is based on a five-year research project conducted under the framework of a succesful grant application by the editors to the Arts and Humanities Research Council (2004), which posed the following question: Is there a future role for craft? It is also based on our work as craft practitioners; Louise's as a textile designer with 15 years' experience in applying her design thinking across a spectrum of creative and management activities and, Georgina's work as an enameller specialising in plique-à-jour for over 30 years.

Until recently, the many fundamental writings and publications on the crafts have been confined to craft as skilful making, largely discussing material, technical and social attributes of the object or final product, be it textiles, ceramics, jewellery, for example. Arguably, this stems from the Arts and Crafts movement in the late nineteenth and early twentieth centuries which brought to the public's attention contemporary crafts[1]. Many historians of art and design (for example, Alan Crawford, Elizabeth Cumming, Annette Carruthers) have treated the period as an object of investigation; however, the practice of crafts as an investigative set of intellectual and practical tools, *ie* a driver of cultural development and change, remains to be established.

The grant application argued for the value of craft to be considered as a concern for innovation, individual vision, intrinsic values and future cultural concerns: a fusion of art, science, engineering, and technology. It posited the practice of craft as a journey through the mind, reliant on building an individual vision through tacit knowledge and, it called for the missing skill of coherently expressing the intellectual and personal voice within the development of work to be filled. It explored craft practice as a socially interactive process (despite being a predominantly individually executed product), where dialogical methods expose contradictions and nurture mindful interrogation: a system of thinking.

The Past, Present and Future Craft Practice (PPFCP) research proposal also acknowledged there was a significant decline in the importance of crafts internationally. This phenomenon was attributed to two mutually reinforcing causes: problems associated with economic viability of producing crafts in a market geared to mass consumption and the decline in quality of existing practice, albeit with notable exceptions (Florida and Tinagli, 2004).

PPFCP asked: What can be learned from historical craft ideologies and philosophies? Why is there a lack of understanding regarding the principles of craft? Culturally, how do crafts relate to the other visual disciplines? What is the value of craft to the development of culture? How does a craftsperson communicate the knowledge embodied and embedded in craft? What is the significance of the craftsperson's approach to thinking for other knowledge domains? How can the discipline of craft regenerate itself?

This synopsis of the original grant application sets the context for the book, which seeks to reveal different facets of the one dialogue, namely Past, Present and Future Craft Practice; a dialogue which is very much alive and continues to be nurtured through close relationships with fellow craft practitioners, academics, public sector bodies and their audiences. This book brings to the reader and to the craft community some of the key insights that have been acquired at Duncan of Jordanstone College of Art and Design, University of Dundee, Scotland. It studies historical and practical craft knowledge; conducts comparative research on visual and cultural aesthetics of craft practice and offers new visual methods of interrogating the process of craft practice for the study of craft knowledge.

Notes

[1] Scottish examples of practitioners from the Arts and Crafts movement include Charles Rennie Mackintosh, Phoebe Anna Traquair and Robert Lorimer. Also in relation to Scotland and the importance of the movement (and vice versa – the importance of Scotland to the development of the movement) it is important to note that the second Arts and Crafts congress was held in Edinburgh in 1889.

Further Reading

Florida, R. and Tinagli, I. (2004) *Europe in the Creative Age.* Carnegie Mellon Software Industry Center and DEMOS.

Jorunn Veiteberg

Jorunn Veiteberg lives and works in Bergen, Norway and Copenhagen, Denmark. She completed her MA in art history in 1982 and PhD in 2000. She has worked as a critic, curator and head of arts in Norwegian Broadcasting/Television and was editor-in-chief of the Norwegian art and craft magazine *Kunsthandverk* from1998 to 2007. Alongside a range of scholarships she was awarded the Torsten and Wanja Söderberg Prize as critic/writer in 1999. She has been a member of Think Tank, A European Initiative for the Applied Arts since it was founded in 2004 ‹http://www.thinktank04.eu›. She is currently Professor of Curatorial Studies and Craft Theory at Bergen National Academy of the Arts. In 2008 she became the project manager of Creating Artistic Value, a research project that will take place over three and a half years. It focuses on the development, during the past twenty years, of rubbish and found objects becoming more commonly used as a material in ceramic practices. The project will unfold through internal seminars and international conferences, exhibitions and publications ‹http://www.k-verdi.no›. Latest books include: *Craft in Transition*, 2005, *Kim Buck – It's the Thought That Counts*, 2007 and *Ambrosia Tønnesen – Stenhugger i det Fine*, 2009.

Georgina Follett

Professor Georgina Follett is a Deputy Principal of the University of Dundee and Dean of Duncan of Jordanstone College of Art and Design. She is also Principal Investigator of the Past, Present and Future Craft Practice, Arts and Humanities Research Council (AHRC)-funded project (£442,306).

Georgina is a contemporary visual craft practitioner of 40 years, specialising in plique-à-jour enamelling. Born in London, she is a graduate of the Royal College of Art. Her practitioner portfolio specialises in plique-à-jour enamelled jewellery in precious metals: a system of using enamel within jewellery to give a stained glass effect. She is the only practitioner of this way of working in the UK and one of a handful in Europe. Her work is held in many private collections as well as the permanent and Roy Strong collections in the Victoria and Albert Museum, and the National Museums of Scotland.

Georgina Follett is a panel member and reviewer for the AHRC Art, Design and Media. She has been actively involved in numerous advisory committees throughout her academic life and is an indexed member of the Crafts Council. She is a Fellow of the Royal Society of Arts and Manufacturers, The Chartered Society of Designers and a Founding Fellow of the Institute of Contemporary Scotland. In 2007 Georgina Follett was awarded the OBE in the Queen's Birthday Honours.

Elizabeth Donald

Elizabeth (Liz) Donald as a mature student gained her Honours Degree and Masters qualification. This experience and her personal background of living and working in South Africa brought a very distinctive perspective to her work as a textile designer, that of the value of craft as a sustainable and economically viable practice from which third world nations could engage in a valuable dialogue on craft practice.

Liz joined Past, Present and Future Craft Practice project in December 2005, seeking to use her professional knowledge to advance the understanding of practitioners and their professional development of their work. This has manifested itself in an Advanced Practice Model (APM) which is the focus of her doctoral studies.

Richard Carr

Richard Carr is an academic and journalist with some fifty years' experience. He is well known for his monologues on craft practitioners drawing the public's attention to the wealth of practice that went under the banner of craft. Richard has also championed within the press the role of the small independent producers of high quality works. This role as an advocate for crafts has been the central tenet throughout his career; his writing has featured in the most prestigious publications associated with craft, *The Guardian* and DESIGN magazine 1970–76. Richard's journalistic career started in the 1960s where he initiated the craft debate as a critic on the *Oxford Mail*, his commitment to writing on craft has ensured that it remains in the public eye as objects worthy of the public attention.

Richard joined the academic community of Duncan of Jordanstone College of Art in 1976; his primary responsibility was to bring into the practice-based programmes the historical underpinning, required as a result of the Coldstream report and the migration of the art and design sector from diplomas into degrees. He continued throughout this period to be an active force for the crafts expanding his portfolio to embrace *The Scotsman, Glasgow Herald, Craftwork, ArtWork, Design Week* and *Crafts*, acting as Scottish Commissioning Editor of *Crafts* from 1989–91. Richard's reputation for craft writing led him to become Scottish Correspondent for *Building Design*, London from 1976–2000. Today, he writes about crafts for *ArtWork* and *Studio International*.

Louise Valentine

Louise has worked in a number of professional environments all associated with teamwork and using design methods as a holistic tool for generating change in organisations. Louise undertook the role of Post Doctoral Researcher within the multidisciplinary team project investigating, 'Past, Present and Future Craft Practice' (PPFCP). This role of understanding change in the context of a team underpinned the project. Louise developed the key public engagements associated with the research bringing into being a conference, symposium, expositions and the establishment of a Scotland-wide Craft Festival by engaging with all the professional agencies in Scotland.

Louise has extended her mindful inquiry (PhD 2004) to establish a methodological approach to understanding the individual creative process embodied within the object. This formed a critical engagement with commissioned practitioners in PPFCP, where she visually mapped the holism of craft to understand the individual optimum circumstances for practice, in order to identify periods of transition and change, individually and at a group level.

Louise is a researcher and academic who has combined these two roles to integrate change as a continuum within the learning and research agendas; her aim is to achieve a productive and generative role for change and its methods and approaches. She is an executive member of the European Academy of Design and a Fellow of the Royal Society of the Arts.

Fanke Peng

Fanke Peng's experience has been gained from studying in different cultures and disciplines, fashion (undergraduate, China) and interactive media (Masters, Scotland). Her PhD, (awarded 2010), developed a new model, VAM (Visual Analysis Model), for the reading of the visual language of craft. The VAM builds the synergies associated with eastern and western cultural philosophies, and provides a holistic model from which to understand language of the craft practitioner.

Fanke is developing her international portfolio through publishing and presentations at conferences and exhibitions, including the Crafticulation and Education International Conference of Craft Science and Craft Education, Helsinki, Finland; the 4th Annual DesignEd Asia Conference, Hong Kong, 2008; the D2B2 – Tsinghua International Design Management Symposium, Beijing, China in 2009; the Hyper Design Exhibition, Shanghai Biennale, China. 2006.

Paul Greenhalgh

Paul Greenhalgh is Director and President of the Corcoran Gallery of Art and the Corcoran College of Art and Design, in Washington DC. His previous posts include the President of Nova Scotia College of Art & Design (NSCAD) University (Canada), and Head of Research at the V&A Museum in London. He has published numerous articles and books, including *Ephemeral Vistas* (1989), *Modernism in Design* (ed.) (1993), *Art Nouveau 1890–1914* (ed.) (2000), *The Essential Art Nouveau* (2000), *The Modern Ideal* (2005), and *Fair World: A History of World's Fairs and Expositions, from London to Shanghai, 1851–2010* (2010).

Frances Stevenson

Frances Stevenson is a studio textile designer operating her bespoke practice from Scotland. She has built her practice from her experience of working at the Crafts Council, London, selling and marketing her work at international venues and trade fairs as well as through the gallery environment. This knowledge has been formative in developing her role as a senior lecturer in Textiles at Duncan of Jordanstone College of Art and Design, University of Dundee. Stevenson has developed a concern for the professional development of practice in order to retain and establish new products for market that sustain and develop both practice and the economic wellbeing of the company/practitioner.

These concerns have manifested themselves through the construction of a PhD study that explores the territory of strategies for embedding professional development as part of practice, ensuring that the objects of practice act as the catalyst and focus, using audiences to engage with the process of product evolution. The aim is to establish Participatory Craft as a product development method for professional makers of contemporary craft, and it explores a practice-based method of innovation for mid-career makers of contemporary craft.

Ian Fillis

Ian Fillis is a Senior Lecturer and Director of Research in the Marketing Division of the Stirling Management School, University of Stirling. He has been involved in researching crafts for over 15 years. Projects have included the examination of craft internationalisation process, image, reputation and identity issues, as well as three socio-economic surveys of the sector in England, Scotland, Wales and Northern Ireland. This work was funded by Arts Councils, Crafts Councils, Scottish Enterprise and Craft Northern Ireland. Ian is also an internationally recognised researcher of small business, creativity, marketing and entrepreneurship. He has investigated the impact of aesthetics on marketing and leadership processes, the tension between artistic and product orientation, the connection between craft and tourism, the use of metaphor, research methodologies and the impact of e-business on small enterprises. He has international links with researchers in North America and Europe and has co-authored papers and a book on entrepreneurial marketing and creativity with Professor Ruth Rentschler from Deakin University, Melbourne. Ian also spends time visiting art galleries and museums and previously worked in an arts centre before embarking on his academic career. He has even held several exhibitions of his own artwork.

Martin Woolley

Professor Martin Woolley is currently Associate Dean of Research at Coventry School of Art and Design. He has previously worked in a senior research capacity at both Goldsmiths College and the University of the Arts London. With an early background in industrial design, his research interests have broadened to encompass new product development, the crafts, environmental sustainability and user-centred design. He has supervised and examined numerous research degrees and been active on many national and international research bodies. As a Fellow of the Royal Society of Arts his contribution has included writing the 'Design Directions' Sustainable Design brief for three years and chairing the judging panel. He was Principal Investigator on two major projects – AGORA, an EU Fifth Framework project which focused on sustainable pedestrian routes in major European cities and 'The Emotional Wardrobe', a Designing for the 21st Century research cluster project jointly funded by the Arts and Humanities Research Council (AHRC) and the Engineering and Physical Sciences Research Council (EPSRC) which examined the interpersonal communication potential of smart textiles and sensor technologies. He previously directed the Higher Education Funding Council for England (HEFCE)-funded 'Demi Project' which established extensive sustainable design learning and teaching resources for UK universities on the Internet. He was the academic consultant to the Design Council's web-based, 'Knowledge Cell' project, supporting the editing and authoring process across an extensive range of web-based information resources intended for business, practice and education. He has conducted design research consultancy for a range of international academic institutions. His personal research interests include how the craft ethos can influence other disciplines, and the ways in which new manufacturing technologies can simultaneously address mass, low volume and one-off production.

Acknowledgements

There is a range of exceptional people and organisations to be thanked for helping bring this publication together. Firstly, the Arts and Humanities Research Council (AHRC) as without their financial support the research would not have been possible. Special thanks go to Ninian Crichton Stuart and Helen Lawrenson for their intellectual and organisational assistance when working with the House of Falkland, which was a central tenet of the research. National Museums Scotland for their expert knowledge and advice which has made the process of publishing an easier task to complete, in particular Director of Publishing Lesley Taylor and Senior Curator of Applied Art and Design, Rose Watban. Grateful thanks to the authors for sharing their craft studies and supporting the advance of craft research by contributing to a series of writings we hope you will find both inspirational and useful as a research tool.

Producing this book would not have been possible without the work and patience of copyeditor Kathleen Brown at Triwords; designer Andy Rice at Not Just Design; and Publication Co-ordinator Vicky Hale; their individual and combined efforts are greatly appreciated. Thanks must also be extended to Ruth Watson and Blair Robertson.

This publication is one of the many outcomes of Past, Present and Future Craft Practice, a major research project based at Duncan of Jordanstone College of Art and Design, University of Dundee. It received support from a number of staff at the University, in particular Paula Francis, Stephen Partridge, Peter Peek, Murdo MacDonald, Bill Nixon, Mike Press, Diane Scott and Sandra Wilson. Finally, as well as receiving funding from the AHRC the project has received invaluable financial assistance from the Scottish Arts Council and Glover to which we extend our sincere thanks.

Introduction
Louise Valentine and Georgina Follett

The development of academic research has brought to the fore a new generation of craft practitioners and as a consequence new methods and methodologies, which are impacting on the way craft in the future will be perceived, marketed and purchased. In the UK the Arts and Humanities Research Council has been instrumental in this transition, as has the commitment of individuals (people and institutions) to engage in this step change for craft.

Reflecting on issues relating to the sustainability of craft practice and its development in the context of culture is not a new activity but the framework of academic research brings a dimension that is new. It offers new ways of discussing craft and highlights a refined definition suitable for the twenty-first century, thereby creating a firm foundation for future practice.

The need to capture this contemporary form of practice, namely craft research, and the emergent craft professional, the 'researcher practitioner' is necessary if we are to continue progressing. There is an exigency to capture the dialogue in dedicated volume(s) of writings rather than a single or a few writings embedded in a volume of research writings committed to art and/or design. In doing so, we address the imbalance in our communication of contemporary practice and contribute to a future dialogue about the sustainability of craft as a sector and a discipline. While participation in the larger artistic and creative dialogue is critical, greater knowledge and understanding in relation to self is also fundamental to growth. It is in this context efforts are needed, particularly if craft is to realise its potential in terms of, for example, knowledge transfer and inter- or transdisciplinary team working.

Craft's recent period of fragmentation which emphasises material specialism and its associated technical attributes led to it being primarily perceived and understood as skilful making rather than an intellectual activity. Material and technical mastery are important components, however the driver of craft is vision and concept. In this context we find craft's second challenge: the division of practice into a series of sub-categories, for example, ceramics, jewellery and textiles. This division celebrates difference yet the principles of practice underpinning them are arguably the same. The recent fashion to differentiate via material speciality exacerbated craft's intellectual capacity and association.

This new series of writing on craft studies brings together contemporary craftspeople, educators and historians from Europe and the USA and represents a sample of the dialogue that has taken place over the five-year Arts and Humanities Research Council project. Each chapter is concerned with the development of craft practice in the twenty-first century; they look at the notion of change but from different perspectives. Individually and collectively they encourage debate. They expose and articulate issues currently being investigated via doctoral research, postdoctoral research, curators, historians and practitioners and, document new ways of questioning and disseminating the dialogue of craft practice.

The opening chapter from renowned European curator and critic Jorunn Veiteberg is a keynote speech given at the 'New Craft – Future Voices' conference in July 2007 (organised by the editors as part of the Past, Present and Future Craft Practice (PPFCP) research). In it Veiteberg boldly advocates that it is becoming increasingly difficult to employ fixed, internal criteria for what makes craft 'craft'. Given the diversity that currently prevails with respect to the use of materials and ways of working, she posits that it has become impossible to uphold a view of craft that is based on clear definitions of goals and means, or as a history characterised by uninterrupted and logical development in which new directions arise as further development of a shared legacy or tradition. Whether this situation means the end of craft, or an expansion of the concept of craft, is an important question open for discussion. This chapter focuses on contemporary strategies that challenge established conventions in the crafts concerning materials, working methods, quality criteria and aesthetics. At the same time these radical approaches have resulted in a revitalisation of the craft scene (in Norway specifically) – just as much through the objects they are making as through the discussions they are raising.

Distinguished jeweller and plique-à-jour enameller Georgina Follett's view of craft is that to be a contemporary practitioner the visual is supreme, with the indexical mark (which offers insight into the practitioner's intellect *ie* their conceptual capabilities) governing the decision-making process. She understands craft as the scientific examination of techniques, technologies and materials harnessed through the indexical mark of an individual producing unique knowledge and insights via a lifetime journey of practice. Follett offers insight into communication of craft thinking from the perspective of the practitioner; offering the title of 'Visual Craft Practitioner' (VCP) as it encapsulates all the areas of craftwork that can potentially influence the work of a visual practitioner. The meaning of this term unfolds as she talks through the background and context to her life as a jeweller, sharing the strategies she employs when working with the generic issues that are central to her craft, namely, nature, colour and the material 18-carat gold. Follett discusses the impact of academic research on her craft methodology and discloses the insights and visual knowledge gained, and the results in terms of the development of her craft practice. She concludes by arguing that a research methodology for practice for practitioners remains unresolved. If the sector is to expand its intellectual growth the need for craft to find a methodology that advances individual practice, and visibly develops and evolves the products of practice, must be met.

Georgina Follett, Louise Valentine and Elizabeth Donald take us on a visual journey through the House of Falkland in Fife, Scotland. The house was a central tenet of the original PPFCP research proposal as it is a virtually undiscovered resource offering an unspoiled interpretation of craft and, it formed an important case study within Donald's doctoral research. Although well known to those who study the buildings associated with the Bute family, the house and its crafts have had little public exposure. This unique resource enabled visual analysis and cultivation of the crafts from a historical perspective. Most importantly it offered an opportunity to have an intimate discussion about craft practice through observation of historical examples in their original environment. In this discussion the authors expose historical craft practice as an intimate dynamic story between different characters (rooms) and their personalities (visual content). The craft of colour, concept, light, marquetry, placement and space, for example, are explored by sharing the whimsical, humorous, shrewdly intellectual, spiritual and delightful narrative that is embodied in the house. The authors suggest that in creating a visual journey the craftsperson allow viewers to experience a variety of elements that are characteristic of the outside world inside the house. She closes by noting that the craft in House of Falkland is an example and demonstration of the intellectual rigour of the creator of these crafted spaces which has not been previously recognised.

Design Historian Richard Carr has a deep and sustained knowledge of how practice and practitioners have evolved over five decades. He has watched the rise of crafts in the 1960s and 70s, followed by a slow decline as design became the 'it' discipline. In his chapter he offers five categories of patronage that have contributed to the development of crafts in Scotland since the end of World War II, namely Architectural, Aristocratic, Ecclesiastical, Governmental and Public Sector. His discussion traces how the Council of Industrial Design and the Scottish Office in London initially led patronage of the craft. That was followed by the setting up of the Scottish Crafts Centre in Edinburgh in 1951 before official patronage was devolved to a number of Scottish agencies. The chapter generally describes the role played by architects working for major Scottish companies, the aristocracy, church and public institutions in Scotland making reference to specific individuals and their craft practice. In doing so, the chapter offers a means with which to increase awareness of the pace of progress and understanding of the nature of the relationship between craft, culture and society.

For Louise Valentine, understanding craft as a form of 'Mindful Inquiry' is a necessary new position as it enables knowledge and understanding of craft in the context of uncertainty, indeterminacy or change; offering a new way of analysing and evaluating craft practice. As part of this research, a historical understanding of craft is required to understand the wider context of contemporary practice and the implications of context for the future. The historical backdrop to the critique of contemporary practice can be linked to the hermeneutic viewpoint of mindful inquiry as an essential level of interpretation, giving us understanding of how the past influences our present thinking. Historical understanding can also be linked to the role of critical social theory within mindful inquiry. In this craft research the role of critical social science is to support examination of the cultural, economic, and political aspects of history in relation to the development of craft. It is to understand how craft as a discipline can support and develop communication of its value and meaning in contemporary society. The chapter is divided into two parts, the first part provides a general view of craft history between 1850–2005; the intention is to provide a context for developing understanding of contemporary notions, views and examples of craft from the period 2005–2010 which is the focus of the second part of the chapter. In closing the chapter posits a frame of reference for future craft practice.

Fanke Peng provides insight into her doctoral thesis where she identified and sought to redress the deficit of visual methods for visual analysis of craft practice. Her research sought to establish a systematic visual analysis model (VAM) for understanding the visual thinking (philosophical and aesthetic qualities) in craft practice. The theory of her exploratory model is applied to craft objects in the field, more specifically, to a single case study based on the life and works of Phoebe Anna Traquair (1852–1936). Traquair was one of the leading craft practitioners in the Arts and Crafts movement in the later nineteenth and early twentieth centuries. The quality of her work and the complexity of the subject matter make Traquair an ideal subject for this exploratory model. Her work has previously been analysed from historical and cultural perspectives but thus far, there has been no attempt to visually analyse her craft or to explain it from the perspective of visual intelligence. The objective of this test study is to focus on the first-hand experience of visually analysing historical craft practice. This provides a discourse to complement existing historical and theoretical approaches to appreciating craft, for example, those presented by Elizabeth Cumming. In essence, Peng's chapter offers insight into the value of the VAM, in understanding the craft practitioner's personal philosophy and aesthetics.

The world renowned curator and scholar Paul Greenhalgh's chapter, (also a keynote presentation at the 'New Craft–Future Voices' conference in July 2007), candidly notes the craft world has been, more or less, in a perpetual combination of intellectual confusion, ideological chaos and institutional collapse for at least four decades. Greenhalgh argues that as a category within the visual arts it has stayed alive largely for negative reasons: nobody has managed to convincingly reallocate the practices contained within it to another category within the arts. He notes that a significant percentage of practitioners who are positioned within the crafts are actually ashamed to be so defined. In itself this is a unique situation in the nomenclatic heritage of the arts. Less depressingly he notes that for some twenty years now, craft has had radical elements within it, which indicate that a new and vibrant role could exist for an intellectually invigorated and technically reformed craft practice. For the first time in decades, craft might be a good naming word. It was this once before of course: the Arts and Crafts Movement at the end of the nineteenth century gained international credence because it addressed the exponential social, economic and political changes of the day. Artistic practice – across the board – began to appear in the twentieth century with Victoriana appearing to the population mid-century. The crafts, if they engage with what we might term the new humanism, could transform themselves. In essence this chapter speculates on the future use of the term craft.

Scottish printed textile designer Frances Stevenson has journeyed as a professional crafts maker within Gallery territory for 15 years. The journey has been difficult at times, as maintaining a balance between sustaining the creative spirit and nurturing innovation within a commercial environment was sometimes problematic. Stevenson wanted to diversify her practice from 'scarves and ties' but found no clear route to take. It was a matter of timing. The maker's creative cycle of inspiration, internalisation, development and realisation seemed out of step with commercial demands. This ultimately led Stevenson to question how craftspeople work and whether there were alternative working models that would help maintain aesthetic integrity and drive innovation without losing the essence of craft. In this chapter, Stevenson initiates discussion about the development of a new paradigm for craft practitioners. The Participatory Craft Practice (PCP) approach is explored as a method of innovation for mid-career contemporary craft practitioners. The model focuses on the development of new products and advocates that new ideas and fresh insights can evolve at the development point of a craft practitioner's progress through participatory activities, rather than solely through individual pursuit. The chapter begins by giving an account of the 'traditional' three-phase craft process (Kettley, 2005) and progresses to presenting four prototypes that have been undertaken to develop and refine PCP. In closing she suggests PCP as a potential innovative method of new product development, for makers of contemporary craft.

Ian Fillis, a marketing academic who has written extensively on craft business(es) as a microenterprise, is concerned with the issue of internationalisation, specifically how artistic and entrepreneurial competencies contribute to business development. He suggests one way of understanding how these factors are operationalised is to construct profiles of the behaviour of people working in craft enterprises. Fillis opens by providing a general view of the literary landscape before explaining the methodological framework to his study. A craft typology is constructed with three key issues, namely motivation, philosophical conflict and, marketing/entrepreneurial interface competencies. Using the data which showed that a variety of beliefs, attitudes, behaviours and orientations were exhibited across the sector, a triangulation process was used resulting in the interpretative construction of four orientations of people working with craft. Each orientation is illustrated and discussed, revealing there are those individuals who have chosen to work in the industry because of the importance of the lifestyle quality involved. Another type of individual is the business-oriented entrepreneur. The third form is described as an artist/designer and, the fourth type enters the industry much later than the other groups. In conclusion, Fillis suggests that those working in the craft sector can be viewed as an example of successful entrepreneurial marketing practice in organisations operating on very limited budgets; they are able to differentiate themselves in the marketplace and achieve competitive advantage through application of creativity of both thought and practice.

Martin Woolley continues the discussion around craft business by focusing on clarification of value and values of the crafted object. He reviews contemporary UK crafts in relation to current socio-technological contexts, in order to identify some of the generic qualities of craft objects. Woolley describes the limitations of our current understanding of these contexts and systematically defines the added value implicit in craft objects, in comparison with their mass-produced counterparts. Through discussion, the general failure of the contemporary craft movement to engage with the 'elusive niches' of the mass market is partly explained in terms of the poor communication of value indicators to a wider public. He argues that one of the overriding values of the craft object is the integration of design and production to form a fused continuum sustained by a unique skill-base, in contrast with the historical dissociation of the two in the case of mass-produced objects. Woolley establishes a taxonomy of these 'value indicators' and creates a model to prioritise and explain their individual significance and interrelationships. The resulting hypotheses are tested through the systematic analysis of individual craft examples, both contemporary and historical. The results are reviewed in relation to the original value indicator model and methodological strengths and limitations are clarified. In conclusion, Woolley discusses how a more informed and strategic debate might be engendered and informed by the findings. This might, in turn, support a more conscious articulation and manipulation of value indicators by practitioners, in order to improve the societal positioning of contemporary craft.

The ten chapters present a complex picture of both the environment within which craft operates as well as the intellectual debates surrounding a discipline that must reinvent itself to ensure its longevity in the lexicon of visual practice – art, craft and design. Craft has travelled down the centuries and has productively led a number of debates; it is now when change is endemic in every aspect of life that the distinct values and methodology engaged by craft have the ability to be anchored in the future.

Changing Craft
Jorunn Veiteberg

Transcript of Keynote Presentation to the New Craft – Future Voices
International Conference, 4–6 July, 2007, University of Dundee, Scotland.

If you had visited the National Museum of Art, Architecture and Design in Oslo in the summer of 2007, you would have been able to see 'The Garden'. It was made, or perhaps we should say woven, by the textile artists Astrid Løvaas and Kirsten Wagle. The materials used were nylon stockings, rainwear, cotton canvas, rags, paint and yarn. Textile materials and techniques are two of the core areas in the discipline we call craft and Løvaas and Wagle's work echoes this tradition.

To be more precise, in this case, their work was inspired by a tapestry by Frida Hansen, who is regarded as the first studio crafts maker in Norway. At the Exposition Universelle (World's Fair) in Paris in 1900, Frida Hansen's work attracted a great deal of interest, not least with portières such as this, which were presenting something completely new in their day, just as Løvaas and Wagle's use of nylon stockings and clothing could also be said to do.

In calling Frida Hansen a studio craft maker, I do so on the basis of the following criteria – she was responsible for the whole process, from idea to finished product; she did the weaving herself and she regarded her portières as unique pieces of art with only one of each of them being produced. Their size, combined with the active exhibiting of her work, went beyond the constraints within which other women remained, in terms of textile handicraft at that time. Frida Hansen managed to support herself by means of her art and she was, in fact, a professional craftsperson.

Even though Løvaas and Wagle's interpretation of Frida Hansen's stylised, yet at the same time, precise, floral motif, is a very free one, their piece is also an example of how artists build on each others' work and thus create a recurrent thread running through the history of textile art and tapestry, from the past to the present.

The textile thread is, nonetheless, merely one aspect of this piece. Its expressive style, in which the different elements can be compared with brush strokes, also gives rise to associations with painting or to be more precise, with abstract expressionism, from Jackson Pollock onwards.

A third approach is the one chosen by the National Museum of Art, Architecture and Design in Oslo, where the piece, 'The Garden', is exhibited among visual art on the theme of art and everyday life. It is next to, for instance, a painting by the Swedish artist, Anders Widoff. The grid is a well-known modernistic theme but the pattern in 'faded' green colour also reminds us of tablecloths, which brings back memories of the archetypical Swedish home in the 1950s. The same applies to one of the other nearby paintings by Sverre Wyller, which combines cardboard from packing cases with strokes of paint applied using a putty knife. What these works of art have in common is respect for the material and physical, the given and the ordinary.

At the Museum of Contemporary Art in Oslo, Løvaas and Wagle's textile work is part of a dialogue around current strategies in painting and fine art while similar works by them are also to be found among craft and design objects at the Museum of Applied Arts in the same

Figure 1. Ineke Hans, 'Big Baskets', 2006. White coated metal frame, pink cord. Courtesy of Ineke Hans

city. This mobility between categories and institutions is not unique for Løvaas and Wagle's work; it is also true of a great deal of contemporary craft and this is what inspired me to begin my book, *Craft in Transition* from 2005, with the question, The End of Craft?

Using many examples from contemporary craft I demonstrated that, what is referred to by the term craft has been so open and malleable that the old lines dividing craft, fine art, and design have lost their meaning. More and more, people feel that these traditional categories are too narrow, a fact illustrated in a highly literal manner by Freddie Robins in a knitted banner, where the answer to the text's question, 'Do I Fit In?' must be, 'No', because the text does not fit into the frame. In the country of my birth,

Figure 2. Hella Jongerius,'Giant Prince' 2000. Ceramics, embroidery. Museum Het Princesseh of, Leeuwarden. Courtesy of Hella Jongerius.

Norway, it is particularly the boundary dividing studio craft and fine art that has disintegrated. In the Netherlands, on the other hand, it is the dividing line between craft and design that is being explored. Furniture and objects by Bertjan Pot, Ineke Hans (*Figure 1*) and Hella Jongerius (*Figure 2*) abound in references to craft techniques; they often require a great deal of manual work, or they are made as unique objects. They, nonetheless, define themselves as designers. 'Craft is about cherishing the beauty of material', said Ineke Hans to *Crafts Magazine* in 2007, adding, 'I like the specific qualities of materials but I like to use them as an industrial designer.

Figure 3. Bertjan Pot, 'Tiger Vase', 2004. Courtesy of Bertjan Pot.

What I'm dealing with is production technology' (Fairs, 2007). Or, as Hella Jongerius puts it:

> I am a designer. Craft is a theme in my work.
> Mixing it with industrial process is like mixing
> high and low tech, mixing first and third world
> cultures, mixing tradition with the contemporary
> languages, different ages and techniques.

She also adds, however, 'For me a designer is a maker. It's like ping-ponging between the head and the hands' (Helgeson, 2002). Here, it is craft in the sense of handicraft that is the theme.

It is tempting to take a pause at this juncture to discuss the stereotypical connotations of her use of the term 'craft', but in this context, the point is the result of her and her colleagues' work. Many of us would claim that their hybrid objects as being just as much craft as they are design. For example, the black vase (*Figure 3*), by Bertjan Pot, which was inspired by a tiger; 'I've seen vases with tigers printed on them, I've seen vases with a tiger skin pattern, but I never saw a tiger jumping through a vase. I tried to freeze that action I never saw' he says, regarding the background to the distinctive shape of this vase ‹http://www.bertjanpot. nl/tigervaseframeset.html›.

Perhaps we should thus conclude that craft has realised its full potential, as it is no longer limited to the form of production and ideological thinking that came with the concept of 'studio'. It manifests itself in many different places and in many different forms. For, in addition to the fact that craft has merged with fine art and design, it has also merged with architecture.

To return to Løvaas and Wagle with whom I started, they were occupied, on and off for four years, adorning the facade of the opera house in Oslo (*Figure 4*). The total surface they worked with was approximately 6000 sq. metres and the material consisted of sheets of aluminium. Given their roots in textiles, they chose to take an old weaving pattern from a weaving handbook as their point of departure. Patterns created for tea towels and other everyday textiles were transferred to concave and convex shapes that create an active interplay between light and shadow on the white facade. This transference is, of course, based on computer technology. The old confrontation between the handmade and the mass produced is irrelevant here and computer technology, which is far too often allowed to serve

Figure 4. Løvaas & Wagle adorned the facade of The Oslo Opera House. Courtesy of Løvaas & Wagle.

as a symbol of alienating technology in the rhetoric of craft, is what creates a surface that radiates visual digitality but which, at the same time, has strong textile properties and a textile content. As one critic maintained, 'It doesn't break down boundaries, it *expands* them' (Strømodden, 2006) and there is a significant difference in this distinction. My keyword today is precisely that – expansion.

In this there lies a certain contradiction of my earlier statement that we are facing the end of craft. I would like to uphold my claim that the diversity that prevails today with respect to the use of materials and working methods has made it impossible to maintain the perception of craft as a discipline based on clear definitions of means and end or as a history characterised by uninterrupted and logical developments in which new schools arise as a further development of a shared legacy or tradition. These kinds of perception and narratives should be considered as being outdated. It was a similar acknowledgement that formed the basis of the philosopher Arthur Danto's famous essay in 1984, 'The End of Art', (Danto, 1984) and that inspired me to indicate a parallel development in craft.

There is, however, something about this thinking that can easily ensnare us. I fear that all the talk about the end of craft can lead to craft dissolving itself and just becoming part of the larger categories of visual art and design. Is this where we want to end up? Has craft's victory literally led to its own demise when an institution such as the American Craft Museum changes its name to the Museum of Arts and Design or when a ceramicist's MA Certificate does not say a word about ceramics or craft but instead, mentions either visual art or design, as is the case in Norway. I want there to be room to discuss issues of this kind; a room offered by this conference which is also an expression of the fact that in today's visual culture, there actually is a separate craft field in the sense meant by Pierre Bourdieu. I, therefore, no longer wish to contribute to the repetitive trope in conversations about craft that it is 'finished', 'concluded', 'terminated' or 'eliminated'.

As already mentioned, I find it more productive to use terms such as expansion and change, when talking about contemporary craft. Thus, I have replaced Arthur Danto with the art theorist Rosalind Krauss as my source of inspiration. Her article, 'Sculpture in the Expanded Field' (Krauss 1979; Krauss 1986) arose from the discovery that the most surprising and contradictory things and phenomena such as land art and video installations, went under the name of sculpture but the conventions associated with the medium of sculpture and which of course were historically determined, did not suit these forms of practice. Established definitions were quite simply unable to encompass them and Krauss, therefore, proposes that other concepts can be just as useful but she also acknowledges that it is impossible in this expanded field to find unifying definitions. The postmodern practice she describes is governed by a logic that encompasses terms that are apparently completely contradictory, for example nature–architecture or unique–reproducible. It is a practice that allows artists to switch between different positions, not allowing themselves to be categorised on the basis of a certain medium or a certain material.

The parallels to ongoing debates and recognisable features of contemporary craft should not be difficult to draw. In the following, I would like to present you with some practices that, in part, insist on craft being their field more or less, but which at the same time, with respect to working methods and the objects they make, will represent an expansion of the field.

The keywords when it comes to working methods are fellowship and interactivity. Many practitioners who have made a mark in the last decade work in groups, in which case

Figure 5. WeWorkInAFragileMaterial, 'Happy Campers', Skylight Studios, New York, 22–23 May, 2006. Photography: WWIAFM. Courtesy of Jakob Robertsson.

they exhibit under a joint name, which entails the individuals remaining anonymous. The choice of names is often highly expressive, for example: Uglycute, Extra Struggle, Temp, Bliss, Revolution on Request, Third Hand and Idiots, which tells us about something that is both yes and no or in-between or that does not quite adopt a stance or allow categorisation. The names also mark a clear distance to the rhetoric of smart design and advertising agencies. We find the same ambiguity that these names evoke in their objects and installations. Temp, which consists of four women who trained as ceramicists in Bergen, called one of their pieces, 'Temptation Island'. They threw everything from design classics to cheap mass-produced dishes and their own unique art objects into a heap. Together, this formed a gigantic mountain of pottery shards – a monument or an anti-monument, a tribute or a protest? The piece is ambiguous, but, at the same time, it represents an accumulation of collective and individual history.

In Western thinking, the artist is a unique figure; she is the prototype of the individualist. These groups, on the other hand, build on fellowship and sign their work as a collective. They emphasise values such as being with each other and being in common, thus challenging not merely the contemporary tendency towards individualisation but also our social structures. Figure 5 shows the group, WeWorkInAFragileMaterial (WWIAFM), in action. It consists of ten Swedish ceramicists and glass artists. They all have individual careers, but many of them spend most of the time on joint projects – such as the one shown at a design fair in New York in 2006. Instead of promoting finished products, they involved themselves in a creative experiment that was about participation: they sewed a troll in three days and invited the public to take part. It was the process itself that was the point. The end product ended up on the rubbish dump.

Unlike the two groups I have already mentioned, most of the groups have members with different backgrounds. The Finnish group, Revolutions on Request, consists of a gold smith/visual artist, an architect, a visual artist and a graphic designer; the Swedish group

Uglycute, consists of two visual artists, an interior architect and an architect, while the three members of the Dutch group, Idiots, have backgrounds in fashion, design, craft and visual art. It is clearly pointless to draw sharp dividing lines between different disciplines in such multidisciplinary milieus. Similarly, the breadth of disciplines represented in such groups leads to greater variation in the materials used.

In several of its projects, WWIAFM has drawn the public into an active participatory role. This also applies to Clare Twomey (*Figure 6*), even though the situation we face in the encounter with a floor covered in porcelain tiles is a different one. Here we are given a choice between being audience or participant. It is the choice we make that is the subject matter of the piece. We are the content; it is our action that activates the piece and it is under our weight that it comes into being. It is a striking thought that art can, in this way, disintegrate under the weight of its content. In its stable, stationary form it is incomplete, while life and movement means its downfall. At the same time, however, the physical experience of feeling the work of art shatter under the soles of our feet emphasises the distinctive characteristics of the material – it is hard but also fragile and fleeting.

Figure 6. Clare Twomey, 'Consciousness/Conscience', 2003. Photographer Andy Paradise. Courtesy of Clare Twomey.

The expectation of a bodily investment in art is characteristic of installation art. More than other genres, installations are about making us conscious of how the art is placed in the room and about getting us to react physically to it. This form of time-based, site-specific and situation-based interactivity is one of the phenomena that represents an expansion of contemporary craft. Interactivity has, of course, always been part of craft in that objects and textiles have been produced for use. This applies, not least, to jewellery, which has a particular intimate connection with its user. But, so far, discussions about this dimension of jewellery have usually been about what happens once the piece of jewellery has left the hands of the jewellery artist and the owner or user takes over. There are, however, examples in jewellery art of people being drawn into the creative process itself, resulting in new forms of fellowship.

The point of departure for the piece shown in (*Figure 7*) by the Dutch jewellery artist, Ted Noten, was a commission from a bridegroom. He simply wanted something beautiful he could give to his bride on their wedding day. Noten wrote a letter to the family and friends of the couple and asked them to send to him one of their own gold (or fake gold) rings, which would form a part of the bride's dowry. This resulted in 56 different rings, varying in quality and beauty. They were all cast in acrylic and became part of the transparent handbag she carried on her wedding day. A book accompanied the bag-jewellery in which the contributors had written down the story or memory that was attached to their gifts and what the connection was between the rings, themselves and the bride. In this way, the dowry also became a story about the function of jewellery in our culture as a gift object and a symbol of the emotional and social ties between people.

Traditionally, craft has been defined through categories of materials, such as ceramics, textiles, metal, glass and wood. These categories are, however, both being challenged and expanded in contemporary craft. Uglycute mostly makes furniture from chipboard. A nest of tables, for example, was made to replace the traditional plinths in an exhibition. Chipboard is cheap and it is also a democratic material, composed as it is of chippings from all kinds of different wood. Chipboard is also part of Uglycute member, Andreas Nobel's table 'Garden Design'. It is a table that nods in all directions at one and the same time, among others to Carl Malmsten (1888–1972) through the leaves that are glued to the tabletop. As some of you might know, Malmsten is one of the key names in Swedish furniture production, and his pro-duction was characterised by a nature-based philosophy. In other parts of the table there is reference to traditional handicrafts, *eg*

Figure 7. Atelier Ted Noten. 'Ageeth's Dowry'. Amsterdam, the Netherlands. 1999. 56 gold rings and other paraphernalia cast in acrylic, pearl/PC. Dimensions: 18x25x8cm. Photographer: Ted Noten. Courtesy of Atelier Ted Noten.

Figure 8. Erlend Leirdal, 'My first day in Helsinki, installation, found objects', Gallery NORSU, Helsinki, 2006.
Courtesy of Erlend Leirdal.

the marks whittled with a knife on the tree trunk that forms the leg of the table. But the use of chipboard would have been banned by both high and low craftsmen and probably also by everyone else who makes furniture from natural materials. This deliberate affront to so-called good taste is, nonetheless, just one aspect of this piece of furniture. More importantly, it is confronting the modernistic perspective that has dominated the discourse about craft for far too long and which entails a one-sided focus on form and the reworking of the material and where the traces of the work process itself are the actual content.

Few people are challenging this paradigm more clearly than the Norwegian, Erlend Leirdal, a maker who also uses wood as his material. The pieces of wood that hang on the wall shown in (*Figure 8*), however, were all found in one day, while wandering around Helsinki. They have not been reworked, simply arranged. Craftsmanship, which so far has been a key measure of quality in craft, thus becomes irrelevant. The same applies to Gustav Nordenskiöld's utility objects, even though the tool he uses is his own body (*Figure 9*). Do we sense here an ironic riposte to all the talk about craft makers' knowledge being embedded in their bodies? Even when his objects contain traces of the work of his hands and not just his head, Nordenskiöld's ceramics have little to do with classic craftsmanship and technical mastery. This type of work represents a tendency that we can call the aesthetics of the random and the imperfect. The products of the British duo, Fredrikson Stallard, also fit in well with this trend. 'Dead Vase', is the title of the porcelain cadaver shown in Figure 10. By consciously exploiting the pitfalls inherent in the ceramic production process, they have succeeded in producing uncountable faults and cracks, thus, each vase in the series is unique. According to what they say themselves, they are balancing on a knife-edge between the traditions of the past and the dreams of the future and with a healthy disregard for the conventions of both.

Figure 9. From Gustav Nordenskiöld's exhibition 'Smash hit!', Svensk Form, Stockholm 2006. Courtesy of Gustav Nordenskiöld.

Few objects address this attitude more clearly than the furniture and lamps produced by Lagombra, a Swedish word that means 'good enough'. The artist behind this company name is Anders Jakobsen. He likes to call himself a radical carpenter and the things he produces are truly radical. For example, a sofa is put together from two plastic chairs from IKEA, which are designed by the well-known designer Thomas Sandell – an example of appropriation craft! It has been upholstered in a pretty rough manner using foam rubber mattresses, while his chandelier has been put together from lamps, sieves, dishwashing brushes and other household objects from IKEA's assortment.

Figure 10. 'Dead Vase', porcelain. Design: Fredrikson Stallard. Individually handmade limited edition of 30. Courtesy of Fredrikson Stallard, London.

This type of object does not just go beyond categories such as design and craft but also those of mass production and unique objects, good and bad, valuable and worthless; they are both yes and no and neither nor but more than anything else, they present themselves as intermediaries between these extremes and opposites. They thus, completely live up to the logic that Rosalind Krauss argues applies to the sculpture in the expanded field.

Another perspective on these works has to do with the role of the user or consumer. Lagombra's furniture points to a new and creative role for the consumer, in which the consumer does not slavishly follow IKEA's instructions but becomes a kind of producer themselves. This remixing of relatively cheap materials challenges many traditional values and virtues in both craft and design, not least as regards concepts such as beauty, functionality and quality. In my eyes, however, this freedom of attitude and action has primarily given the field a new vitality.

Like Ted Noten, Lagombra uses ready-mades in his work. For some people, ready-mades represent the limit of what craft makers can use as materials, if craft as a concept is to survive. I, however, am not one of them. I believe that there is a field of research here that will demonstrate that in craft, ready-mades work on several levels. For example, they are often used to create links to, or shed light on, the history of craft and its categories or materials. In the hands of the craft artist, ready-mades are a material on a par with any other material but they carry within them memories and meanings from the contexts of which they have previously been part. In that sense, they help to clarify aspects of things that are highly relevant to craft as an object-based discipline. Quite simply, craft's roots and materials and making constitute a very interesting context for ready-made objects. In addition, the use of ready-mades also builds bridges to studies of material culture and ensures a wider horizon for understanding than that offered by art history and design theory alone.

The introduction of mass-produced and anonymously-designed products into craft and their subsequent transformation into unique art objects, patents a completely new kind of craft. In these objects, the old oppositions of industry, design and art form part of a new order within one and the same object. Yet another example of forms of practice that have expanded the field.

The perspective I have chosen here is neither new nor original but it has informed most of the debate about craft in the past decade. It is perhaps more new that the debate has spread to more areas of art and culture, thus underlining that this expansion of the field is continuing. One visible indication of this is the term, 'designer-maker', which is becoming increasingly widespread. A glance at the 2007 summer exhibition programme also reinforces this impression. At the Museum of Contemporary Art (MOCA) in Los Angeles, for example, they presented the exhibition, 'Poetics Of The Handmade'. This exhibition presented artists from Latin America who, based on their interest in 'transformation and process', have formed works of art with their own hands. 'They have found poetry in the depiction of quotidian objects and in the powerful resonance of small actions,' as it said in the press release at the time ‹http://www.moca.org/museum/exhibitiondetail.php?&id=384›. Their actions require both patience and manual dexterity and the interesting thing in this context is whether it is not precisely such virtues that we admire most when we encounter such works of art?

The Swedes take a more aggressive approach and have launched a new concept, *formhantverk*, which translates into English as 'crafted form'. This took place in connection with an exhibition called 'Hands On Movement − Crafted Form in Dialogue',

Figure 11. WeWorkInAFragileMaterial, Röda Sten, Gothenburg 2005. Video still.
Photography: WWIAFM. Courtesy of Jakob Robertsson.

shown in Stockholm. The curators of this exhibition were Zandra Ahl and Päivi Ernkvist, whom some of you probably know as the leaders of the Craft in Dialogue project. For these two, the time for manifestos is not past. For them, crafted form is a separate movement, 'Crafted form cannot be defined as design, craft or art; instead, it is a phenomenon that is engaged in dialogue with these genres,' (Ahl and Ernkvist, 2008) – entirely in line with the rhetoric that applies in the expanded field. Furthermore, the content of the concept must not be mistaken for an aesthetic-formalistic programme:

> *Unlike traditional crafts, romanticising of technique and materials, crafted form emphasises communication, questioning and experimental production processes. (Ahl and Ernkvist, 2008)*

This covers the kind of craft I have presented to you.

It is no longer of value to attempt to delineate craft to certain tools, techniques, materials or medium-specific conventions. The expansion of the field has led to a situation in which none of these traditional parameters remains intact. But there is much that needs to be addressed, both of a historical, ideological and aesthetic nature.

In the meantime, we can allow ourselves to be informed by what the makers are creating and by how they, themselves, understand their role. WWIAFM has produced an information film with which I would like to conclude. It is not an educational film about the work process from A to Z, on the contrary, it takes an ironic look at craft's allegedly fetishist relationship with its materials in addition to indirectly providing a humorous answer to a certain media cliché concerning the portrayal of craft makers. We are familiar with this cliché from articles in the glossy magazines. Set in a leafy garden in some out-of-the-way location, the maker poses with a ceramic dish on her lap – there is nothing wrong with this but it represents a very romanticised picture of the maker's work. WWIAFM's film is about an urban workplace where the workers' clothes get stained and the hands get dirty, but which also offers fellowship and the opportunities for various kinds of expression. The music and choreography are borrowed from Kylie Minogue's video, 'Slow', but instead of Kylie and a thousand sexy dancers on a beach, we meet ten[1] craft artists at work and in life-affirming dance (*Figure 11*). If these are not the future voices of craft, they are certainly among the more vital voices on the contemporary scene.

Notes

[1] In 2007, there were ten members. One has since left the group.

Further Reading

Ahl, Z. and Ernkvist, P. (eds.) (2008) *Crafted Form: Continuation, Praxis and Reflection.* Stockholm, Vulkan.

Danto, A. (2004) The End of Art. In: Lang, B. (ed.) (1984) *The Death of Art.* New Haven, New Haven Publications.

Fairs, M. (2007) Burning down the divide. *Crafts Magazine,* 205, 38.

Helgeson, S. (2002) Hand och huvud. *Form,* 4, 35.

Krauss, R. (1979) Sculpture in the Expanded Field. *October,* 8, 30–44.

Krauss, R.E. (1986) *The Originality of the Avant-Garde and Other Modernist Myths.* Cambridge, Massachusetts: MIT Press.

Museum of Contemporary Art, Los Angeles. (2009) *Poetics of the Handmade.* [Online] Available from: http://www.moca.org/museum/exhibitiondetail.php?&id=384 [Accessed 3rd March 2010].

Pot, B. (2010) Tiger vase. [Online] Available from: http://www.bertjanpot.nl/tigervaseframeset.html [Accessed on 3rd March 2010].

Strømodden, J. (2006) Harder stuff Løvaas & Wagle's decoration of the opera house at Bjørvika. In: *Løvaas & Wagle.* (2008) Oslo, Nasjonalmuseet for kunst, arkitektur og design. p. 115.

Figure 1. 'Bluebells'. The enamel is a singular colour, which provides a harmony to the piece, as the forms of the flowers are of a scale that to hold a colour variation would disrupt the overall imagery.

Visual Craft Practitioner
Georgina Follett

What am I?

Defining my profession is not an easy task. There are those who may see me as a Jeweller. However, I only possess some of the skills that are associated with jewellery making. Others may see in my work the skill of an Enameller. But calling me this fails to encapsulate the dynamics of the profession I belong to, as the skills I have in this area are limited to only two types of enamelling. Complicating matters further I can also be considered a Goldsmith as the material I choose to work with is 18-carat gold. Yet as I work with other materials this title does not define me. Simply put I am all and none of these things, a hybrid not easily defined or categorised (*Figures 1, 2 & 3*). This trait I suspect is true of most of my profession as we collectively produce work that is both independent of typecasting and not easily cloned. When taking these factors into account it makes the title of 'Visual Craft Practitioner' (VCP) seem somewhat appropriate as it encapsulates all the areas of visual craftwork that can potentially influence the work of a VCP.

Becoming a Visual Craft Practitioner

The visual craft profession demands that its advocates are people who constantly seek to understand visual development through practice. In turn, this generally means that the skills associated with trade develop over a great deal of time.

In my case, the first stage of this development came during the eight years I spent in education. In the beginning much of what I produced during my college years was consigned to the bin. The work more often than not resulted in a clumsy attempt to articulate a visual theory in a poorly conceived manner that lacked any real hint of imagination. I simply did not possess the necessary skill to carry off many of the complex ideas that underpinned these visual theories. Nevertheless, despite these early frustrations I was able to try and test many different forms of practice, understand my visual fascinations, play with ideas, and remain outside of the public eye until I had both the confidence and the body of work that I felt could be placed within the public domain without compromise.

Once my work reached the public domain I did not allow this to affect the body of work I created and continued to produce work that satisfied my own personal goals, as opposed to the needs and desires of others. However, it is important to note that I selected this strategy not to satisfy some overwhelming desire for self-satisfaction but because to do so would most likely have had a detrimental impact on the continuing development of my work. Clients tend to like the work to remain similar and to have an influence on other people so that it is profitable in the market. Therefore, in order for my work to be accepted it would be necessary to obtain a market which like all markets would be dependent on stability of product. In turn, this would restrict the development of my work because I would have to continually produce similar products and as such would be unable to constantly seek to push myself beyond my knowledge limits and use each piece to move forward an element of exploration. By resisting the temptation of trying to create such a niche market for my products I have been able to continually develop the work I produce. My refusal to lower my expectations by settling for a narrow field of competence has allowed me to continue to push the ideological content of my work. In fact, it is this very refusal that has allowed me to forge a strong relationship between me and the materials and techniques that have supported my work (*Figures 1, 2 & 3*) and created the unique visual language that has been distinctive of the crafts I have produced over the past forty years.

Material Choices: metal

For a VCP selecting a material to work with is not a trivial matter of random selection based on material value or a fleeting sparkle that attracts one to an object like a magpie to a shiny coin. On the contrary, it is a carefully considered choice that arises gradually over time and eventually allows the VCP to identify the material that has the capacity to underscore the visual forms that they seek to achieve.

Despite a range of catastrophes experimenting with material that has occurred during my career, there comes a time when one develops a strong and somewhat sentimental attachment to their material of choice. I have the most symbiotic relationship with 18-carat gold. It has a number of notable qualities that make it particularly useful for the crafts I produce. For instance, 18-carat gold allows me to work with the finest wire which holds its form even when soldered. Unlike other metals which require silver solders to bond them together 18-carat gold has its own solder. This factor is particularly crucial as using a silver solder carries with it certain inherent limitations. When used on non-silver metals silver solders will often leave blobs of other colours that damage the finished product. Furthermore, even when it is used on silver it tends to blob and flow unevenly. In turn, this requires an inordinate amount of cleaning which, coupled with the fire stain problem[1] associated with silver, leads to contamination of the enamel colour and ultimately a loss of form. By having its own solder which is indistinguishable from the metal itself 18-carat gold overcomes these limitations. Moreover, the higher melting point of 18-carat gold relative to other metals[2] ensures that the visual form of jewellery is left intact as the metal flows perfectly and requires the minimum cleaning at the final stages of construction.

In short, for me, 18-carat gold is a dream as it both tolerates my visual requirements and has a number of positive attributes that make it simple to work with. I understand how to form the material manually and it responds to my particular way of manipulation by working with me rather than against me. In turn, this means that it requires the minimum amount of

Figure 2. 'Random Chance'. The colour palette is vibrant and the greens are purposefully selected to 'throw' the red hues forward. Colours are arranged through a methodology used to replicate the randomness of nature.

Figure 3. 'Violas' is a combination of enamel on metal and plique-à-jour, where the intention is to 'throw' the red hues through the yellow gold base and use the deep purple transparent centres as recessive colour to draw the viewer's eye inward. Previous examples of work in my portfolio focused on the form whereas the intention was

struggle to achieve the results I desire when fabricating. This factor is critical as to struggle and force a material to behave against its nature (as often happens when manufacturing) can only be achieved with the most sophisticated technology. Moreover, in order to be economic this technology has to run continuously or it is not viable. Not only do I not have the financial reserves to run such an operation but the entire manufacturing process leaves me feeling somewhat dislocated from my work and frustrated with the outcome. In fact, in order to be satisfied I need to be in control of an idea from concept to product.

Enamelling

For me colour is an addiction. In order to create the visual images that I seek, colour is always a must and without it I become visually bored. However, the limited colour range of red, yellow, white and green offered by metals alone fails to encapsulate the true nature of the visual image I seek to create. This means I must seek out other materials to combine with metals to improve upon the range of colours offered by the quiet restrained palette of metal alone.

When adding such colours to jewellery I am presented with a variety of options. Plastics offer a vibrant choice. However, they are subject to certain limitations as the plastic is a separate element from the metal itself and the techniques of bonding the two materials together is subject to a short lifespan[3]. Resins too offer a complete range of colour. However, they are generally fluid materials that require boundaries within which to sit. In addition, they are deaf to form and can only be transformed by machining or casting; both of these processes I find alien, as they do not allow the natural characteristics of the material to be retained. Moreover if you affect their natural process and force them into artificial forms they are unpredictable in their use and will often deteriorate quickly.

Enamelling as a discipline is often considered one that most individuals with any degree of sense should strenuously avoid. The material itself is surrounded by myths that tell tales of a substance that is impossible to work with because of its unpredictable and idiosyncratic nature. To those who had never used it, enamel was seen as having the potential to dismay even the most dedicated of craftsperson and none but the selected few that had been endowed with the special gift to understand its deeper complexities should dare to use it. Thus with a considerable degree of apprehension that I would become one of the many professional casualties that enamel indiscriminately left in its wake I began to experiment with this perilous material. However, after working with it I soon realised that these myths were exactly what they claimed to be; in that they were myths.

I discovered quickly that when I used transparent enamel that allows the light to permeate the surface of the enamel the colour was second to none as it gave the finished product an overall visual intensity that ensures even small areas of colour are given the maximum possible impact. In addition, I soon realised that when placed directly onto the surface of 18-carat gold the enamel complements the yellow colours of the gold in a fashion that resonates the colour of both materials. Nevertheless, despite the evident advantages of this it is necessary to be careful as unless the correct balance is struck between the two materials the base metal colour will reflect through the enamel and restrict the ability of certain colours to stand out by turning them into shades of turgid grey. In order to overcome this problem, most enamellers will apply a base flux which seals the colour of the metal surface and allows the enamel to vibrate colour. However, in my opinion there are disadvantages to this technique as it requires the application of a greater depth of enamel and any wires that are introduced onto the surface to key the enamel into place and prevent it cracking lead to a poor visual effect.

In the past, to overcome the inherent disadvantages of this technique, I have generally selected one of two strategies. The first involves carefully selecting colours of enamel that will be enhanced by the yellow base of the gold when applied to its surface area. Failing this, in situations where I wish to use colours that will not be enhanced by the yellow base of the gold I generally use a technique known as *'Plique-à-jour'*[4]. This technique was invented by Benvenuto Cellini[5] and involves using enamel like a stain glass window, which allows light to penetrate straight through it. However, despite the practical benefits of this technique it is often avoided by many in the profession. Whilst it is possible to find examples of plique-à-jour in the literature[6] the principles of this most useful technique are not expounded. Closer examination of current examples in the literature[7] reveal that in most cases, due to the absence of technical instruction, the enamel is often placed on a bed of mica. Whilst this allows for filling in the 'window' (enamel) which creates a well-finished front surface it generally results in a back surface that is flat and not contoured which gives the finished piece a feeling that seems to lack an overall harmony.

Once I had decided to use this technique I quickly discovered that there was a complete absence of any professionals with the necessary skill or knowledge of plique-à-jour to educate me in the finer points of this rare form of craft. This factor meant that if I ever wished to attain the necessary skill to master this technique I would have to do so through my own merit. This point of realisation signalled the beginning of my long journey of testing and refining a method of employing enamel that eventually allowed me to create the visual image that I desired. Obviously when doing this there were a number of failures; however, over a significant period of time my efforts paid off and I managed to develop a technique that continues to allow me to create a uniquely balanced and vibrant colour-effect in the jewellery I produce[8]. At this point it is important to note that I do not claim to have mastered this technique and I am continually building this knowledge and my own confidence in employing it as a tool for creating the crafts I produce.

Overall, the main advantage of this technique for me is that it does not constrain the forms I develop and it allows me to create three-dimensional, curved or multiplaned enamel that can be applied to the crafts I produce. Moreover, the work now has the potential to become large scale; the technique has the capacity to create three-dimensional durable forms that will stand the test of time and last for generations to come. This of course is the goal of most VCPs. When creating crafts in general VCPs strive to create a product with a visual image that is so alluring to its viewer that the product will echo across time. For the VCP it is not about creating a fleeting transient form of expression that lasts only for the moment; on the contrary it is about creating a visual image so potent that its legacy will have a lifespan that far exceeds that of its creator.

Source Material for Idea Generation

A VCP's inspiration may come from many facets of life. There are those who seek inspiration from architecture whilst others will take it from nature. For me I have always been in the latter category. In particular, flowers have always intrigued me. Their colours, forms, life cycles and fragility continue to amaze me. I love both the panoramas they create and their individual detail. In fact, for me when I gaze over a green field and catch the various points of colour that are spread across the horizon, the view is second to none. For jewellers I believe this relationship stems from a need to decorate the human body in the same way that flowers decorate the landscape.

Moreover, the range of inspiration that is derived from flowers is almost as diverse as the plants themselves. Different types of flowers have their own unique stories to tell. Forget-me-nots speak of love whilst jasmine represents purity, honesty and faithfulness. In my own work I often find that working with a single plant as a source of inspiration allows me to focus on the essence of that plant and reflect this in the crafts I produce. Here it is important to recognise that I do not literally translate the images of these plants in the work I create but instead use them as a tool to provide a series of images that encourage visual exploration in terms of colour, form, patterns and tone.

Idea Initiation

Once I have found my inspiration the next stage is to translate this inspiration into a concrete idea. This is a process that I consider very carefully, as once committed to an idea I find it impossible to leave it behind. For me to do such a thing would seem like admitting defeat and make me question my own judgement.

To begin with it is important to recognise here that this process of idea initiation is by no means a simple one and contrary to popular belief it is not possible for a VCP to simply catch a stray pearl of wisdom that allows for the creation of an instantaneous and useful idea. In fact, the first stage of this process often takes a great deal of time. There are occasions when I will take years to study a plant in order to watch it grow in different lights and different surroundings. Over time I will take visual notes concerning different aspects and details of the specific characteristics of the plant and this, in turn, will furnish me with a greater understanding of its visual potential as a tool to understanding the perspective from which I am going to approach the piece[9]. Thus at this stage, by considering various points of analysis such as the colour palette of the plant, growth patterns, and the relationship between its various constituent parts, I gain a greater understanding of its overall structure which then provides me with a basis for understanding the visual elements that I will include in the piece. However, it is important to note that this does not necessarily define the overall form of the piece.

Idea Development

After the basis of an idea has been formed, much like the plant that inspired the idea, it requires nurturing to allow it to develop into a piece of craft. Over the years I have developed a tried and tested working method which involves continually moving between materials, techniques and drawing to refine and define the formal elements of construction that strongly dictate the outcome of the piece. Here, I generally work using an additive process as over time I have realised that employing a reductive strategy too early in the conceptual process has had a detrimental impact on the finished piece. Thus to avoid this type of error I am exceptionally careful to retain as much visual information throughout the early stages of the process and leave the removing of surplus elements to the later stages.

Obviously when developing such pieces there are a variety of factors to take into account. By far the overriding consideration relates to the scale of the constituent elements of the plant in relation to how they will be reflected in the piece. For instance, in reality a plant may have very small or large flowers which would become disproportionate if translated literally into metal form. In order to overcome this problem it is often necessary to scale certain elements of the plant up or down. However, this is much easier said than done. To take something from the natural world and alter the relationship between its elements often causes considerable visual displacement. Moreover, unfortunately it is almost impossible to foresee these displacements prior to their occurrence. This means that to ensure the piece has integrity considerable care must be taken to realign the relationship between these elements to ensure that the appropriate visual balance between them is struck.

Once the correct scales of the various elements are determined the next stage is to look at the structure of the metal base element of the piece. Here it is necessary to consider the proportion of space required for the various indented patterns that will be inserted into the piece and eventually filled with enamel. This does, however, create a slight complication as it is necessary to consider whether the enamel colours that are applied will function effectively and create the desired visual proportion. For instance, a saturated mid tone of red will hold more visual space within the final piece than a light yellow. In turn, this means that an unequal amount of actual space has to be given to the areas that will hold these two enamels in order to create a balanced visual space between them on the finished piece. Simply stated a greater amount of space must be devoted to the area for the yellow enamel for a balanced visual structure.

This technique may sound simple when explained here, but visualising a piece in this manner is no easy task. It is necessary to visualise the entire form of the finished piece from its metal skeleton by considering how the finished article will look when colour is placed over the metal during the final enamelling process. The problem when doing this is that whilst I usually construct in my mind a viable form for the final piece I have never successfully constructed a piece as originally conceived at this stage. This is because all the original conceptual thinking fails to materialise in the form I originally conceived because it is not possible to retain all of the diverse constituent elements of the piece in the mind's eye. Moreover, drawing or recording the idea to the final stage fails to compensate for the limitations in human recall as the process of conceptualisation cannot be considered independently from the creation of the piece itself. This is because together these elements form a complex process that is subject to continual refinement, evolution and change. At this stage it is important to note that I do not mention this to point out any limitations in the process of creating a piece but instead to note that the gulf between conceiving and constructing a piece is one that is subject to significant modifications that are generally essential if the finished product is to have visual integrity.

Developing the Idea into a Piece of Jewellery

Even though all the stages of the process I use to create any piece of jewellery are of critical importance, without a doubt of key importance is the stage of developing an idea into a piece of jewellery. Bearing in mind that as this stage of the process transforms the piece from an abstract idea to a constructive design, it is hardly surprising that a variety of elements must be considered. Generally speaking the first of these considerations is establishing the specific area of the human body that will give the object the best opportunity to function as a piece of jewellery. This factor is often dictated by the scale of the individual elements of the piece and their relative levels of fragility.

After considering these factors I will often have a good general idea of the final form that the piece will take. I rarely construct something that is an individual element, however, and the piece will often be comprised of a variety –sometimes hundreds – of separate forms. In turn, this means that the construction process is extremely complex. To alleviate some of this burden, prior to the assemblage stage, I will create all of the constituent elements that I perceive as necessary to create the piece whilst also establishing a system of how they will be linked together. Nevertheless, despite these precautions, it is a rare occasion when everything goes according to plan and more often than not I find that once I begin bringing these elements together they conflict with each other or simply fail to articulate the intended aesthetic design. When I bring the piece together I generally work on a model of a human form and it is not until this stage that the limitations of the intended design are exposed. Sometimes I find that the composition aspects are flawed or notice having seen the pieces juxtaposed for the first time that I have failed to give sufficient consideration to the space between the various elements of the piece. Regardless of the nature of these problems, anytime I have begun refining the model on the human form it has become the most difficult aspect of every piece I have ever created. It usually becomes a battle between creator and piece. In the past I have found that in order to create the finished piece it has been necessary to restructure the piece over ten times.

In the early years of my work, in order to overcome many of these problems, my instincts were to make such refinements by using a strategy of random chance. I would work from the perspective of using a dice to decide the order pieces should be formed in the hope that it would reflect the appearance of randomness in colour that seems to run throughout nature. Today, however, when I stumble at this point I seek to use a theory or a method that is distanced from my instinct. If I am unable to find a suitable theory I will simply put the piece aside until I can come up with a solution, as I am no longer willing to seek a quick solution to my problem at the expense of the final piece.

Developing the aesthetic design of the piece in this manner allows it to then move onto a stage where others can view it as an object of desire. This is of critical importance, as once the piece has reached this stage it is finished in my terms as it takes on a new existence as the property of another. Therefore, this means that it must appeal to another in a manner that will allow them to feel confident that the piece will bring them pleasure and reflect their personality.

Reflection on Practice: process and outcome overview

The 'Past, Present and Future Craft Practice' research project offered an opportunity to reflect on my practice and understand craft process in an alternative manner. One of the observations made when comparing a research methodology to a craft practice methodology was that there was a gap, in that a review of the literature was essentially missing from my craft methodology. I sought to rectify this and introduced it as a means of progressing and contextualising my practice. This process required me to reflect on my practice as well as reading the key literature surrounding enamelling and plique-à-jour.

A review of the literature within the domain of international enamelling was the method for understanding the precedence of previous enamel practice and as a means of appreciating where the knowledge gaps were in terms of the visual language of plique-à-jour.

George Fouquet, Peter Carl Fabergé, Louis Comfort Tiffany and René Jules Lalique were identified as key practitioners whose work collectively and individually offered a benchmark for best practice and a suitable framework for the evaluation of my own craft practice.

I conducted an evaluation of my work over a six-year period (2000–2006) by analysing the photographic record of the majority of my portfolio during this period. I visually compared this record of intellectual progression against other items in jewellery publications (Phillips, 2000; Snowman, 1990; Gere and Munn, 1996; Falk, 2004) as a way of providing greater general understanding of the quality of my work relative to that of other individuals in the field (Fabergé, Cartier, Lalique, Fouquet, Traquair). Additionally, it was understood to be a way of gaining insight into my position in the discipline as a whole.

Following this, an examination of the work of other enamellers was undertaken to establish the current position of the knowledge base in the enamelling of three-dimensional forms in order to ascertain if my own work was expanding that base. Through this critique of practice it was discovered that the only significant reference to anyone enamelling three-dimensional forms (for example, 'Arum Pins', as seen in *Figure 4*) dated back to the work of the French jeweller George Fouquet in the latter half of the nineteenth century. However, his portfolio indicated that he had only succeeded in creating parts of a form or undulating elements within his work by employing the plique-à-jour technique. Therefore, his work was limited in this field. Moreover, through analysis of the work of Peter Carl Fabergé and Louis Comfort Tiffany, I noticed that the majority of their work applied enamel to a flat metal surface in order to give it colour. This is a technique I have also employed. However, it is a well-known jewellery method that has been well documented and as such, does not add to the current body of knowledge in enamelling techniques. In short, what seemed to run concurrently through the examination of the literature was that the key elements of the plique-à-jour within any piece of jewellery were few and far between with the exception of those already cited.

The main exception to the apparent absence in the literature of the plique-à-jour technique is seen through the work of René Jules Lalique. Lalique applied the plique-à-jour style extensively throughout his career and his work was selected as a useful comparator to establish if my work was expanding the current knowledge base in the area. When using the technique, Lalique always applied the enamel to a flat surface using large dimension 'cells'. These cells would have been filled using a backing as the front and back surfaces have different surface tensions; the reverse surface flows to the edges of the metal frames and the top surface retains the fluid movements of enamel after firing. Lalique used enamel for the creation of flat surfaces; he never used plique-à-jour to construct three-dimensional forms. In contrast, within my own work I generally always employ a three-dimensional form. This involves using a technique of applying the enamel in a meniscus of water in order to suspend the enamel during the firing process; this results in the same enamel signature on both the top and bottom surfaces of the pieces. To the best of my knowledge this technique is currently used by no other and represents an innovation in the field. In turn, this suggests that my work is expanding the current body of knowledge in the area.

Figure 4. 'Arum Pins' is an example of enamel as structure where the enamel is on a curved surface, giving structural integrity within the overall structure of the piece rather than simply being a decorative element.

Having examined the literature and compared it to my own work, attention was redirected to the issue of form and how the forms used in my work give the pieces an aesthetic quality. This analysis revealed a variety of useful points. The most critical of these indicated that whilst colour, transparency and opaqueness were all key elements that could be associated with my work, I had been using the colour in a very two-dimensional manner. This limitation in my pieces seemed to run through those of other jewellers also − the jewellers (*ie* Louis Aucoc, Leopold Gautrait, Lluis Masriera, Pierre Vever) had simply applied a single enamel colour to the base metal in order to give the finished product impact and richness. However, very few individuals had attempted to moderate colour **over** form by creating a complex visual image that is characterised by various colours **across** the piece. When considering this factor I realised that in my earlier pieces I had tentatively begun to explore this but had failed to carry it forward. This observation provided the base from which to make the decision to explore the opportunity of mixing enamel colour on sheet metal to give a painterly quality to the surface and to examine the light refraction.

Having evaluated my enamelling process I then went on to look at the final forms given to jewellery with an analysis of a variety of work spanning from the now priceless art forms of the ancient Greek and Roman periods to that of my contemporary visual craft practice. Following this I examined my own aesthetic value with specific reference to how I worked necklaces. Based on a comparison between the works of others (*eg*, Lalique, Henry Wilson, early pieces by Watkins and Ramshaw, Cartier) and that of my own I soon realised, to my dismay, that I had fallen into the traditional mirror image method of formation that involves balancing the piece in terms of function by placing equal weight at either side of the central line and mirroring the forms away from this central point. Upon recognising this I determined that my new work would eliminate this cycle of convention that seemed to run concurrently through my work. The next piece would be asymmetrical rather than a simple mirrored reflection from the central line.

Overall, the analysis I had made of my previous work and the relevant materials in the literature gave a clear direction when beginning the crafting of the next new work. The conclusions drawn from this evaluation allowed the key parameters for future craft practice to be established and also assisted in identifying the challenges I would have to address in the making process.

Figure 5. 'Violets' is an exposition of the resolved problems of achieving a painterly effect through enamelling. Enamel is traditionally applied using colours determined by a manufacturer's palette; this is applied to the metal, usually through a single colour. In 'Violets' the green colour applied to the leaves is mixed and blended together to give the illusion of light and shade falling on the leaves, moving the enamel colour from a flat surface to a light-refracting surface. The overall visual effect is one used by painters to give depth and form to surface.

Reflection in Practice: process and outcome overview

The perspective with which I viewed contemporary craft practice was informed by the preference within the literature to highlight craft as a skill set rather than an intellectual act, and the lack of knowledge of craft practice as a methodology; subsequently limiting craft as a service to its sister disciplines, art and design.

This viewpoint directed how the 'present' *or* contemporary craft was studied; it was studied from the perspective of the practitioner *ie* myself. It resulted in the decision to use case study as a vehicle for articulating craft as a methodology while concurrently challenging the intellectual and visual literacy limitations of my discipline (of enamelling) through my own craft practice.

In terms of progressing the intellectual underpinning of my practice, the initial phase of study (*ie* contextual and literature review of historical craft practice, including my own craft practice history) asked the following questions:

- Where would my work be positioned within the niche practice of enamelling?

- Which other enamelled pieces offered insights into the same skill base?

- What technical aspects of enamelling have been explored?

- Is there a gap in knowledge of the techniques employed and if so, where is it?

- Could the(se) gaps in knowledge be filled by the development of new work?

In conducting this review a series of observations around visual literacy within the construction of jewellery pieces resulted, enabling the development of a new visual quality in my enamelling. The key observations were the need for new work to have an asymmetrical composition, to mix enamel colour directly on sheet metal in order to give a painterly quality to the surface and to examine the resulting light refraction.

These conclusions established the key parameters that would define my new product(s) and also assisted in identifying the challenges I would have to address through the process.

Two new pieces of work were the vehicles for articulating craft as a methodology and exploring the visual knowledge gaps in the discipline of enamelling. They were 'Violets' *(2007, Figure 5)* and 'Field of Endeavour' *(2008, Figure 6).*

Reflection on and in Craft Practice

Having adapted the traditional research methods of literature review (from the perspective of the practitioner), via a visual review of the craft practice jewellery, I used this to establish a framework for exploration and innovation within my practice and produced two pieces from the perspective of the craft researcher. This method of approach differed significantly from the methodology taught within the 'Art College', where the frame of reference is the insularity of one's tutors, peers and own practice.

The Researcher Practitioner is a new force for craft (Valentine, 2004); practice as research has always been accepted as a valid research method by the Arts and Humanities Research

Board (later Council), since its inception in 1998. However, models of how to achieve this, and their potential impact on practice, have yet to be established or evaluated. Whilst this advance is visible to the individual, a dialogue needs to be established for the public domain to access visual thinking and visual knowledge embedded in objects.

My 'Holy Grail' for practice is to find a methodology that advances individual practice, and visibly develops and evolves the products of practice. Through my own practice, I will continue to develop a research methodology for practice for practitioners, and develop/ expand intellectual growth for craft.

Notes

[1] Fire stain occurs through the process of heating metal; it brings to the surface of silver a dark grey colour, which is different from the rest of the metal. Removing it through cleaning the metal surface with abrasives deforms the overall metal structure creating undulation on the surface.

[2] Eighteen carat gold has a higher melting temperature than silver and other metals with a high copper content and is therefore less susceptible to melting in the kiln.

[3] Plastics in the form of perspex require gluing into any form; the glue discolours the surface of the perspex and leaves a visible trail. Thus in jewellery forms, this trail can appear to cover a larger area of the material than is free from it. Perspex glued into a structure made of fine wires is inherently vulnerable to breakage, and as such a piece that is worn will suffer from the effects of wear.

[4] "Plique-à-jour" (French, "open braid") [is a type] of enamelling that resembles cloisonné, but differs from it in that the partitions are soldered to each other rather than to the metal base, which is removed after firing. The remaining shell of translucent enamel gives the effect of stained glass. Because it has no metal base [a] plique-à-jour enamel is exceptionally fragile; few early examples have survived.' (Encarta)

[5] Benvenuto Cellini was an Italian goldsmith, painter, sculptor, soldier and musician of the Renaissance.

[6] See for example, Phillips, C. (2000) *Jewels and Jewellery*. London: Victoria and Albert Museum and Snowman, A.K. (ed.) (1990) *The Master Jewelers*. London: Thames and Hudson.

[7] This difference in surface tension was observed through examination of pieces of work in exhibitions; there is no research to substantiate this, purely the visual evidence from the objects of practice.

[8] I am currently unaware of any other VCP that employs this strategy and it is on this basis I claim its uniqueness to my work.

[9] At this stage I will usually generate ideas of the form I intend to give the piece. For instance, I may decide if I intend the piece to take the shape of a necklace, brooch or chain.

Further Reading

Falk, F. (2004) *Schmuck Jewellery 1840–1940*. Germany: Arnoldsche Art Publishers.

Gere, C. and Munn, G. C. (1996) *Pre-Raphaelite to Arts and Crafts Jewellery*. Suffolk, UK: Antique Collector's Club Ltd.

Hoffman, H and Davidson, P. (1965) *Greek Gold, Jewelry from the Age of Alexander*. Germany: Phillip von Zabern.

Loring, J. (2003) *Tiffany Flora and Fauna*. New York: Harry Abrams.

Phillips, C. (2000) *Jewels and Jewellery*. London: Victoria and Albert Museum.

Snowman, A.K. (ed.) (1990) *The Master Jewelers*. London: Thames and Hudson.

Untracht, O. (1982) *Jewelry Concepts and Technology*. USA: Doubleday and Company Inc.

Valentine, L. (2004) *The Activity of Rhetoric within the Process of a Designer's Thinking*. [Unpublished Doctoral Thesis]. University of Dundee, Scotland.

Figure 6. 'Field of Endeavour' is an exposition of
the resolved problems achieving an asymmetrical
composition through form and the application of
mixed enamel colour.

Figure 1. House of Falkland: the house and its landscape were conceived as a single entity, with the interior iconography reflecting much of the flora and fauna found within the landscape.

House of Falkland: a historical case study of Scottish Craft

Georgina Follett, Louise Valentine and Elizabeth Donald

Introduction

House of Falkland is a resource of international significance *(Figure 1)*. The House is an 'A' listed building designed by William Burn (a pre-eminent Victorian country house architect), built between 1839 and 1844 with the exterior and the landscape created by Alexander Roos; the internal decoration commissioned by John Patrick Crichton-Stuart, Third Marquess of Bute, a great Victorian patron of the Arts who installed works by Robert Weir Schultz, Horatio Walter Lonsdale, and others (mainly in the period between the 1910s and 1930s). House of Falkland has never been subject to investigation, nor sought resource support from any public body. As a resource for research it offers the opportunity to have an intimate discussion about craft practice through observation of historical examples in their original environment.

In order to gain an insight into how crafts have evolved into the products of today's practice it is important to see and understand the heritage of crafts practice within the context of the modern world. The crafts of today tend to be singular. In this sense, they have moved away from a constructed interior into portable objects. This is primarily due to the fact that forces such as globalisation have created a more fluid society where people move around more and tend not to be anchored to a single place. Houses and homes have become more transient in people's lives. To compete with these developments in modern living, crafts have evolved into products that are easily transportable, as opposed to those which are integrated into houses and homes. For instance, crafts have tended to gravitate towards personal adornment and objects such as jewellery, fashion, ceramics, and furniture[1]. These types of craft are distinct from integrated crafts as, regardless of their physical location, such objects give their owners a sense of place and stability and can be moved from one location to another on a permanent or temporary basis. In short they travel with individuals and acquire meaning in their lives. The crafts are not mass-produced and are often selected with great care and attention. This process of selection forms a bond between the owner and the given crafts that gradually blossoms and acts as a vessel for memory, celebration, and commemoration.

Exhibitions are now one of the few opportunities to see a volume of crafts coexisting[2]. However, exhibitions rarely construct an interior ambience or ethos. The contemporary craft objects tend to hold their individuality and often fight for attention within the construct of the exhibition. They are rarely quiet in that they act as part of the fabric of a building, in the background, in support of life and living. Moreover, it is also quite rare to see more than a few pieces of work or a body of work by an individual. This creates a significant barrier to understanding the significance and meaning behind a particular piece of craft because created pieces of craft are not singular objects but part of the journey of a practitioner whose commitment is to developing a vision articulated through craft practice over a lifetime. Craft in isolation takes longer to understand. In fact it is exceedingly difficult to give these individual pieces of craft meaning in a vacuum without the luxury of knowing and understanding the place of a particular piece of craft in the lives and homes of those who own them.

Figure 2. Detail of the Corpus Christi frieze around the top half of the wall in Lord Bute's bedroom is in the style of the Pre-Raphaelite brotherhood. The constructed visual effect of the frieze is to ensure that you raise your eyes, and physically turn to follow the procession which fills all three main walls, leaving only the large window wall free.

When considering these salient points in relation to House of Falkland, the significance of the House becomes evident. The fact that the House has not been converted into a public venue but has been left as a private home means that although it has had many alterations over the years, the internal craft has retained the integrity of its original commissioning. In short, the house is sufficiently intact to allow the viewer to identify and understand the original intention of the craftspeople who eloquently constructed the works.

Lord Bute's Bedroom

Nowhere is this eloquence more evident than in Lord Bute's Bedroom, where the Corpus Christi frieze fills the space (*Figure 2*). When the viewer stands in the room everything visual is above eye level. This forces the viewer to raise their eyes upwards and, in turn, this gives the work an emotional feeling of adoration. Looking upwards the first thing that stands out is a magical scene of a religious procession in the Pre-Raphaelite style[3]. There is a constant need to turn to follow the procession and this is only broken by the window which allows the viewer to visually go outside and return back into the room to continue viewing the work.

Underneath the procession there is lettering in gold which goes right around the room underscoring the mural (*Figure 3*). The colour green is predominant across the whole room with gold constellations on the ceiling (*Figure 4*). The imagery is outlined in black and this intentionally gives a feeling of stained glass which reinforces the religious conception of the work. Quiet reflection upon this work reveals that the room as a whole has been dressed with a romantic, fictitious reference to the crusades.

The sides of the room are almost a mirror image but are not sufficiently symmetrical to provide a visual balance which keeps the viewer's eyes moving with the procession.

This means that whilst the visual information has been constructed and composed in a manner that allows the viewer to have a flow of appreciation, this flow is not constant and the viewer will take intermittent pauses to assimilate the information. The interspersed foliage complements this by providing visual rests between the individuals within the procession. To accompany all of this the use of flat paint with little tonal referencing provides an effect that is reminiscent of stained glass; which is by its nature flat in colour and articulated only by light that flows from the exterior. At this stage it is critical to recognise that by relating the imagery to stained glass, the craftsperson has subtly emphasised the religious theme, costume and style in a manner that is closely related to the work of Burne-Jones[4].

The Boudoir

From the Corpus Christi room you walk into Lord Bute's Study and pass through the servants' hidden passageways (*Figure 5*) to enter Lady Bute's Sitting Room or the Boudoir. This room is an exemplar of visual confusion. Craft work upon craft work has been introduced at different periods in different styles by different authors. It does not look to be the work of a single concept but is an eclectic mixture of imagery, textures and colours which leaves the viewer visually confused and overwhelmed almost to the point that they are dismissive of its content because of this visual confusion (*Figure 6*).

Figure 3. Lettering in gold beneath the Corpus Christi frieze.

Figure 4. Gold Constellation on the ceiling of Lord Bute's bedroom. The placing of the heavens above and the deep green colour of the ceiling accentuates the weight of the imagery adding to the visual language in the Corpus Christi frieze. This reinforces the feeling of being in the presence of a greater force through diminishing the viewer's physical body.

Figure 5. Ornate cornices and ceiling in the hidden servants' corridor. The visual language of the garden is brought into the house through the use of the rose; 'under the rose' is to keep a secret, and House of Falkland means 'hidden place', as does servants' corridor. A visual play on words.

Figure 6. Frieze of ships in Lady Bute's boudoir. The ship frieze directly relates to the family's commercial trade. It is incongruous visually and does not sit compositionally with the rest of the imagery within the room.

Alongside this, the miscellaneous mix of visual references surrounding the musical figures in the room, whilst telling a historical story of John Patrick Crichton-Stuart, add to the viewer's visual confusion. These objects are flawless in their execution but lack playfulness. In turn, this suggests that artisans[5] rather than craftspeople constructed them as they lack a visual integrity. The individual and collective aesthetic does not leave the viewer wanting to return to extract their meaning and understand the embedded conceptual message that can only come from frequent seeing and careful looking. They have no intellectual referencing within them; they simply provide a historical and stylistic comment. In short, they lack the coherent and stylistic integrity that is characteristic of other crafts within the house.

Despite the initial perspective of the room, a deep breath allows the viewer to separate the content and to understand the layers of craft within the room. Most of the imagery is flat in plasterwork. The exception to this, and most interesting, are the musical figures which are beautifully worked (*Figure 7*). Their colour is harmonious and is capable of resonating visual sound[6]. By looking at each of them individually in their three-dimensional form, the historical references to ship figurines become apparent as they lean out entering the space of the viewer. They articulate the function of the room and evoke images of the figures in the Palau de la Musica in Barcelona. They have a quality and sensitivity that engage the eye and seek out their individuality whilst simultaneously, and somewhat mysteriously, connecting them one to the other. Additionally, these figures are classical in concept, celebratory, slightly bacchanalian in character, and evocative of fauns, fairies, and elves, those creatures that have the magical capacity to transport individuals to a mythical location of pure joy; a location that allows them to reflect upon what they have seen. This reflection allows the viewer to understand the role of music and its function as a tool to elevate human spirits and transport people to another world that is not confined to the moment.

The Formal Drawing Room

In direct contrast to Lady Bute's Boudoir, the Formal Drawing Room is the most restrained room as formality dominates. Upon entering the room the sheer size and scale of the room becomes immediately apparent to the viewer (*Figure 8*). At this stage it is important to recognise that in the context of the nineteenth century, the purpose of this space was to display the stature of the guests present at the Marquess of Bute's functions and also the finery of the events that took place there.

Figure 8. Ceiling and fabric wallpaper in the Formal Drawing Room. The plasterwork ceiling is following the tradition of Scottish plasterwork used in formal rooms of the period.

Figure 9. Details wood and mother-of-pearl inlay in the walls of the Drawing Room. The inlay of insects is a delightful inclusion into the formal environment of the Drawing Room. The work is of the highest quality as shown here by the selection of the veneer to reflect the birds' plumage.

Figure 10. Wood and mother-of-pearl inlay in the walls of the Drawing Room. The repetition of the 'under the rose' secret meaning reinforces the hidden place meaning of House of Falkland. Combined with the secret lives of the birds and insects, this gives the formal room a playful feel, bringing the outside inside.

Figure 11. Wood and mother-of-pearl inlay in the walls of the Drawing Room. This depicts birds and insects.

The space is complemented by the delicate balance of crafts throughout the room. The wood floors and panelling provide a tonal integrity to the room as a whole (*Figures 9, 10 & 11*). Quiet inspection of this panelling reveals an inlay which discreetly catches the light. Moving closer the viewer sees the most delightfully inlaid forms of birds and butterflies which come in a variety of different woods and other natural materials such as mother-of-pearl. They come in different forms and are at different heights. In fact the detail is such that if the viewer was familiar with ornithology they could recognise different species and identify each form as a sympathetic rendering of the original. There is, however, no pattern detectable to the placing of these forms and to the viewer it seems that they have been randomly placed. Upon noticing these forms the viewer begins to see them everywhere and this, in turn, creates an intimate surprise of individual discovery. At this stage to the viewer it seems that they quietly hide amongst the panels seeking to be invisible to humans whilst discreetly watching humans as they go about their lives.

When taking these various factors into account it becomes evident that the craftsperson who designed this room intended it to reflect an interpretation of nature. The quality of the work is that of a master craftsperson who has a deep understanding of nature and the natural world. The craftsperson clearly has the vision and skill to interpret this image of nature visually without a slavish adherence to photographic representation. They have a deftness of skill; one which seeks only to be used in the service of this vision. Overall the room is flawless in its conception and execution. Quite simply it is a gift for adults and children alike.

The Grand Staircase

The Grand Staircase opens off the hall (*Figure 12*). When looking upon it the viewer immediately becomes aware that the staircase lacks the romantic theme that is characteristic of many of the rooms throughout the House. The staircase projects a dominant masculine image upon those who look upon it. This image, of course, is by no means an accident but an intentional act designed to create a public statement of status and family lineage that reflects the wealth and power of the family who once resided there. Alongside this, the images of heraldry from not only the Marquess of Bute's family but many others[7] also serve as a constant reminder of this statement.

At the apex of the staircase lies an enormous stained glass window created by H W Lonsdale[8]. The light reflects through the window and casts a coloured light onto the stairwell. In turn, this illuminates the stairs in a fashion that displays power. When examining the window in more detail it is evident that this particular piece of stained glass is not a piece of craft, as its design is both formulaic and not open to interpretation. After some consideration, it becomes apparent to the viewer that, as a design principle, the stained glass window serves a single purpose, to obscure the outside world and restrict the viewer's gaze to the confines of the stairwell and landing.

Once the viewer has reached the top of the stairs they find the landing which is dominated by a barrel-vaulted ceiling that is decorated by a series of imagery often associated with the classical themes of the Renaissance style (*Figure 13*). Visually, however, what is particularly striking about these images is that they have been painted using saturated colours. These colours provide an overall feeling of weight, richness and opulence which give the images life and make them feel somewhat heavy and uncomfortable. In turn, this predominant visual weight above the viewer's head seems to diminish the human scale whilst additionally having the effect of emphasising mortality.

After appreciating these features of the landing the viewer's attention is then drawn to the various doors that lead off from it. These seem small in proportion; an effect which is caused by the scale of the barrel ceiling. Entering the door nearest the stairs leads into the Vine Corridor which is the most highly and coherently decorated part of the house (*Figure 14*).

Figure 12. The staircase and barrel-vaulted ceiling use traditional symbolism stating the heritage of the family; their place in society is reflected in the scale of the imagery.

Figure 13. The barrel-vaulted ceiling. The imagery used is again historical contextualising the family's heritage.

ΒΟΡΕΑΣ
ΚΑΙΚΙΑΣ

14

small in proportion to what it is trying to illustrate, a clever combination of detailed imagery complemented by a mixture of natural light, which stems from a series of three copulas, takes the viewer on a whirlwind journey that is symbolic of love and romance (*Figure 15*). The overall visual image the corridor seems to represent is reminiscent of being in an orchard. However, a more detailed description is necessary to do the experience justice.

The walls of the corridor have been skilfully decorated with images of espalier trees with orchard fruits and various small animals, birds and snails among the branches, and a trellis of vines crossing the ceiling from which hang bunches of ripe grapes (*Figures 16 & 17*). The fruits are organised on each branch in forms that are instantly recognisable to the viewer. From a design perspective it is apparent that the sheer density and number of these images create a busy and somewhat overwhelming pattern in the corridor.

The stuccowork is in relief and by giving it three-dimensional form, this has the effect of enhancing each of the images. Moreover, the overall pattern has been organised using a grid system which provides the image with a feeling of visual integrity and affords the viewer clarity of perception.

Alongside this, the natural light that stems from the three consecutive and evenly spaced copulas combines with the images to provide an overall feeling of a day's trip through an orchard. The initial entry into the corridor under the soft blue spectrum of colour of the first copula provides an experience of the beginning of an early morning journey through an orchard. The second leg of the journey is provided by the bright yellow daytime light of the second copula. Then finally the deep red light of the third copula brings the journey to a close at dusk. The coloured lights from the cupolas touch and transform the corridor. A large mirror at the far end of the corridor reflects the imagery and magic of the space. Underlying this journey is a deep sense of symbolism that is reminiscent of what is best described as a love affair. The fruits represented on the trees are symbolic of love, fertility, healing, wisdom and health; all those aspects of life that are sought. The animals selected for the images seem to be those that humans most commonly engage with such as birds, ducks and squirrels. They seem to carry with them a more diverse symbolism, including enlightenment, perspective, prophetic knowledge, longevity, courage, speed, wisdom, the safe return and love of home. At this point it is important to note that collectively these images speak of a bountiful nature.

15

16

17

Figure 14. The Vine Corridor showing its compositional form based on a grid system
with repeated elements creating the overall structure.

Figure 15. Detail of one of the three cupolas representing morning. The colours within the
glass affect the colour of the light entering the corridor taking you from morning to night
via pale blues to deep red hues.

Figure 16. Mice playing amongst the espalier branches in the Vine Corridor. The mice have
multi-layers of meaning in the Vine Corridor. They represent order and scrutiny. They can be
viewed as part of the natural world, amongst many creatures of the countryside. And they are
private playful creatures.

Figure 17. Bunches of grapes hang from the overhead trellis in the Vine Corridor.
The vines form the basic compositional structure of the corridor.

Most significantly, it is crucial to recognise that the overall experience the craftsperson provides allows the viewer to experience, even if only for the briefest of moments, the outside world of a daytime journey through an orchard and vineyard inside the confines of the Vine Corridor. This factor is indicative of the outside–inside relationship that runs concurrently through much of the craft in the House.

Exiting the corridor under the red light of dusk from the third copula leads the viewer into the tiny lobby. The lobby contrasts with the corridor because it is much simpler in its form and design. However, at ground level the craftwork is equally if not more significant. Inlaid in the floor are primroses and violets which are two of the first heralds of spring and symbols of love. This imagery is reinforced as they are under your feet, strewn in your path, indicating a deep sensitivity and value given to relationships. The fact that they are inlaid in the floor rather than on the walls or ceiling, demonstrates a level of attention to detail that speaks volumes about the ethos that the craftsperson is seeking to inculcate into the fabric of life as well as the fabric of the building. It is unique to see these patterns inlaid in the floor. Moreover, even though they are common decoration, the images of single plants carry with them a deep symbolic meaning. They have clearly been placed with intention but in a manner that transposes them with simplicity and sincerity. In turn, these factors demonstrate a degree of craftsmanship that goes beyond using simple skill of hand by ascending to skill of heart and mind.

The Master Bedroom

The Master Bedroom is dominated by the ceiling which rises in tiers to its highest point. The first level is decorated in plaster with oak, which is symbolic of protection, wealth, health, healing, potency, fertility and luck (*Figure 18*). The oak is interwoven to give the appearance of a canopy of trees with two squirrels in the branches. At the centre of this image the trees appear to open up to reveal the sky with parting clouds. Together these factors suggest that, to some extent, the room has been designed in an attempt to draw the viewer's gaze upwards.

Figure 18. The ceiling in the Master Bedroom. It is formed of oak leaves which symbolise strength and endurance. Oak is also the tree of doors believed to connect worlds. The visual language used is descriptive of the form of the ceiling with the branches travelling up the sides of the vaulted structure and the leaf canopy flowing over the non-structural spaces.

Closing Comment

Taking all of this into account it is evident that the journey through the corridor, lobby and master bedroom is a wonderful piece of visual storytelling. The narrative is whimsical, humorous, shrewdly intellectual, spiritual and above all family friendly and delightful. In creating this journey the craftsperson allows viewers to experience a variety of elements that are characteristic of the outside world inside the house. They experience not only a journey through an orchard during the three stages of day but are also afforded the opportunity to glimpse a cultivated garden, meadow, and finally a wood with a canopy in the trees that allows the viewer to peer through to the sky. Moreover, the craftwork is loaded with symbolism of a deeply private and personal nature that embodies images that are powerful, spiritual and romantic. It is a demonstration of the deep intellectual rigour of the creator of these crafted spaces which was not previously recognised. Every visit reveals something new. It is a 'magical' place.

Notes

[1] See Harrod, T. (1999) *The Crafts in Britain in the Twentieth Century*. Yale University. ISBN 0-300-07780-7, and Greenhalgh, P. (2002) *The Persistence of Craft*. New Jersey, Rutgers University Press. ISBN 0-7136-5001-X.

[2] The Victoria and Albert Museum in London (2008) *Out of the Ordinary: Spectacular Crafts* and the National Museums of Scotland (2007) *Cutting Edge* are exemplars of these exhibitions.

[3] Marsh, J. (2005) *The Pre-Raphaelite Circle* (National Portrait Gallery Insights). The National Portrait Gallery Publications. ISBN 1-85514-352-6.

[4] Edward Burne-Jones was the leading figure of the second generation of the Pre-Raphaelite Brotherhood. He was a pupil of Dante Gabriel Rossetti and a protégé of John Ruskin. His work contained a narrative style of romantic symbolism steeped in medieval legend and he became one of the most sought-after painters in Europe. He was also a partner in Morris & Co where he was responsible for most of the stained-glass designs.

[5] The term 'Artisan' is derived from the Italian word 'artigiano' meaning a skilled manual worker, and is applied to one who manufactures or crafts items by hand with hand tools as opposed to mass production or industrial production. An artisan was a skilled manual worker, but not normally the designer or the 'brains behind the project'.

[6] Visual sound is a term used here as a metaphor for the levels of intensity in terms of visual content and confusion.

[7] The date at the top of the stained glass window, within the flags, is 1892. It was created by H W Lonsdale. The additional images of heraldry flanking Bute are those of Stormont, Athol, Skene and Bruce.

[8] Horatio Walter Lonsdale was an accomplished architectural artist working as William Burges's right-hand man on many schemes, such as Cardiff Castle and Mount Stuart as well as working in the House of Falkland and Falkland Palace. His attention to detail and colour was held in high regard. His work was greatly admired for its ability to render highly decorative designs.

Patronage and Craft in Scotland: 1945–2010
Richard Carr

Background: cultural, political and social synopsis

When World War II ended in 1945, Scotland was a very different place from how it is today. The war had provided a reprieve for many of the traditional industries that were the backbone of its cities – shipbuilding, steam locomotives, engineering and textiles in Glasgow, for example, and shipbuilding and textiles in Dundee. There was a mixture of hope and decline in the following years: in Glasgow, decline marked by the closure of the North British Locomotive Company in 1962 and the launch of the QE2 which was the last Cunard Liner to be built on the Clyde in 1967; and in Dundee, hope expressed by the new factory for Timex[1] In Aberdeen, it would be more than 30 years before the dwindling fortunes of the fishing industry would be replaced by the arrival of North Sea oil; and in Edinburgh, it would be another five years before the first Edinburgh Festival put the city on the world's cultural map.

Introduction

This chapter makes reference to five categories of craft patronage in Scotland, namely Architectural, Aristocratic, Ecclesiastical, Governmental and Public Sector. However, before looking at these a general overview of 'patronage' is offered.

Patronage throughout the millennia has been exercised by emperors, kings and their generals, the leaders of tribes, clans and religious orders. Wealth and power have been exercised to commission palaces and their fitting out and decoration, equip armies and give presents both to those whom they serve and to those who serve under them. The commissions for armour, drinking vessels and chariots, for example, have usually been found in burial chambers where such items were intended to aid the passage from this world to the next. In the case of the leaders of religions, patronage of the crafts can be found in the temples of Ancient Egypt, Greece and Rome, or in Jewish synagogues, the palaces, cathedrals and monasteries built by popes, bishops and abbots, and the mosques built by leaders of the Muslim faith. Then, as societies became wealthy and more urbanised influential and powerful people, such as local governors, government officials and merchants, provided patronage. Arguably, the greatest of all such patrons were the Medicis of fifteenth-century Florence.

Architectural Patronage

Architects and their clients have played a major role in patronage since World War II, whether undertaking major projects such as the Princes Square development in Glasgow in 1987 or smaller ones such as the conversion of a church hall in Inverness into art.tm in 1998. The former, by Hugh Martin and Partners for Guardian Royal Exchange and Teesland, includes the magnificent Art Nouveau ironwork by Alan Dawson as well as work by John Clark, Jane Muir and Dai Vaughan (Carr, 1988a). The latter, by Sutherland Hussey Architects, is noteworthy for the staircase balustrade by Peter Chang, the cowl at the top of the balustrade by Andrew Tye, door furniture by Wendy Ramshaw, furniture by Mike Malig and

Robert Kilvington, a reception desk and display shelf by David Germond of Juggernaut and crockery by Richard Slee. All the craftspeople were funded by the Edward Marshall Trust (Carr, 1998b, 1998c).

Two major buildings demonstrate how patronage of the crafts by architects and their clients can be exercised on a grand scale. The first is the General Accident Headquarters built on the outskirts of Perth in 1983. Here, the architect James Parr of James Parr & Partners, working with Art in Partnership, used the project to commission a tapestry by Sam Ainsley that concentrates on aspects of the Scottish landscape to depict General Accident's Scottish origins, and batik panels by Norma Starszakowna to celebrate the company's worldwide operations. There is also a mural by Mike de Haan, a brass coat of arms by Bob Hutchinson, and banners by Susie Paterson and Andy Taylor. The tapestry and batik panels were the biggest single craft commissions of their kind ever to be undertaken in Scotland (Carr, 1988b).

The second major building is the Scottish Parliament in Edinburgh, designed by Enric Miralles and opened by Queen Elizabeth II on 9 October 2004. The Scottish Parliamentary Corporate Body (SPCB) established an Art Steering Group, also working with Art in Partnership which, commissioned a number of craftspeople to produce work on the theme of identity and what it was like to be living in Scotland at the time of the commission. Among the pieces are 'Honours of Scotland' by silversmith Graham Stewart; 'Territory – Fields of Endeavour', a gobelin tapestry by Maureen Hodge; 'Hinterland', silk organza panels combining hand painting and digital printing by Norma Starszakowna (*Figure 1*); the oak and sycamore information and reception desks by David Colwell; and the lettercut steel and stone texts located at the threshold of Queensberry House by Gary Breeze. There are other text panels by several Scottish lettercutters, including Gillian Forbes, along the Canongate Wall ‹http:// www.craftscotland.org/Scottish_Parliament_Craft.htm›.

Figure 1. Norma Starszakowna, 'Hinterland', 2004. 18 wall mounted textile panels.
Digital and hand processes printed on silk organza substrate. © Scottish Parliament.
Licensor http://www.scran.ac.uk.

Figure 2. Dovecot Studios, 2008.
Photograph by Shannon Tofts.
Image courtesy of Dovecot Studios.

Aristocratic Patronage

Aristocratic patronage of craft has often been a long-term venture, beginning with Catherine, Countess of Dunmore who set up Harris Tweed in 1842 as a means of bringing employment to the island. The most notable example of aristocratic patronage must be The Dovecot (Edinburgh Tapestry Ltd) that was founded by the Fourth Marquess of Bute in 1912, though the idea for the tapestry weaving workshop was originally mooted by the Third Marquess and William Morris in the early 1890s. From its conception until after World War II, the workshop wove only for the family and its first two weavers came from Morris' own studio in Merton Abbey, Surrey.

After the war, The Dovecot was directed by the founder's daughter, Lady Jean Bertie, who took the workshop into the public realm by using its own weavers to undertake commissions and collaborated with artists such as Stanley Spencer, Henry Moore and Graham Sutherland, creating tapestries for both private homes and public spaces. This policy continued when the Fifth Marquess sold The Dovecot to John Noble and Harry Jefferson Barnes in 1954, when they appointed as artistic director Sax Shaw and then Archie Brennan. Under the former, Tom Phillips designed tapestries for St Catherine's College, Oxford and John Maxwell the 'Cycle of Life' for the Scottish Arts Council, while heraldic tapestries were woven for the Queen Mother. Ecclesiastical commissions included tapestries for King's College, Cambridge and the Church of Saint John the Divine in New York. Artists working with Archie Brennan included Eduardo Paolozzi, Elizabeth Blackadder, Robert Stewart, John Bellany, Alan Davie and Barbara Rae.

Back in Bute hands in 1984, The Dovecot experienced financial difficulties despite prestigious commissions such as that for tapestries designed by Frank Stella for Pepsi Cola's Headquarters in New York and attempts, under the artistic directorship of Joanne Soroka, to diversify. The Dovecot was put up for sale in 2000. Unexpectedly, an Edinburgh businessman, Alastair Salvesen, came to its rescue, appointing David Weir as its director. Even more surprising, after having moved from its original premises in Corstophine to a hut in the grounds of Donaldson's College in Edinburgh, Salvesen and his wife underwrote the entire cost of converting a former Victorian public baths in Infirmary Street, Edinburgh into The Dovecot's new home (*Figure 2*).

3

4

5

Figure 3. Alan Davie, 'Cosmic Signal', 2003. Tapestry woven by Douglas Grierson and David Cochrane. Image courtesy of Dovecot Studios.

Figure 4. Patrick Caulfield, 'Pause on the Landing', 2005. Woven at Dovecot Studios by Douglas Grierson, David Cochrane and Naomi Robertson. Image courtesy of Dovecot Studios.

Figure 5. Lord Bute (Sixth Marquess) and Peter Simpson, late 1970s. Image courtesy of Bute Fabrics Ltd.

The Infirmary Street premises allow for increased exhibition space, one gallery that is devoted to showing tapestries and the other run by Innovative Crafts under the direction of Amanda Game. Tapestries woven by The Dovecot Studios Ltd (its new name) include 'Cosmic Signal' which was designed by Alan Davie (*Figure 3*) and 'Pause on the Landing' which was designed by Patrick Caulfield for the British Library in London (*Figure 4*). A tapestry has also been designed by Victoria Crowe for the Duke of Buccleuch, whose family has been commissioning tapestries since the sixteenth century (Carr, 2008).

The Marquesses of Bute have initiated various new forms of patronage for the crafts over the past sixty-five years. The most notable example is Bute Looms, set up on the Isle of Bute by the Fifth Marquess to provide work for soldiers returning home after the war. Initially a fashion fabrics business, the name of the company was changed to Bute Fabrics in 1975 when the Sixth Marquess appointed Peter Simpson as its design director (*Figure 5*). Saying that it takes seven times the length of cloth to cover a sofa as it does to cover a woman, Simpson saw the company as a supplier of upholstery and curtain fabrics, not of fashion materials, and immediately began designing upholstery fabrics for the top end of the contract market. Clients include furniture manufacturers such as Knoll International, Herman Miller and Steelcase in the US, Fritz Hansen in Denmark, Artifort in the Netherlands and Hille in England. In the 1980s, Bute Fabrics carried out commissions for the Royal Navy, Heathrow Airport Terminal 4 and the new Sheriff Court in Glasgow (Carr, 1987a).

Today, the Bute Fabrics design studio in Rothesay is run by Catherine Murray who works with designers such as Tom Dixon, Jasper Morrison and Barber Osgerby (*Figure 6*) to build upon the collection established by Simpson, some of whose cloths are still in production. They maintain the policy of weaving principally in wool although silk, rayon and elastomeric yarns are also used from time to time. They continue the use of subdued colours whose inspiration is often hinted at by the Scottish names given to Bute fabrics (*Figures 7 & 8*). Just as Simpson experimented with ways to introduce random colours in a manner not unlike Ikat weaving, so Dixon has chosen the colours for a new fabric called 'Storr' based on bouclé techniques. Recent commissions have included providing upholstery fabrics for the refurbished Royal Festival Hall in London and the Wales Millennium Centre in Cardiff (Carr, 1998a; http://www.butefabrics.com).

Figure 6. Barber Osgerby, Skye, 2007. Image courtesy of Bute Fabrics Ltd.

Figure 7. Fabric on rocks, Crail, mid-1980s. Image courtesy of Bute Fabrics Ltd.

Figure 8. Interior Design International Exhibition, late 1980s. Image courtesy of Bute Fabrics Ltd.

Aristocratic patronage can also take a purely financial, but nonetheless very important form. For example, the Sixth Marquess of Bute supported Ben Dawson in the launch of his cabinet and furniture making company in 1986, which has gone on to be very successful, including commissions for the Scottish Parliament (*Figures 9*) and National Assembly of Wales (Dawson, 2010; ‹http://www.bendawson.com›).

The creation of employment has been a popular form of aristocratic patronage and resulted in the formation of Caithness Glass in Wick, which was founded in 1960 by Sir Robin Sinclair, later Lord Thurso. Originally intended to supply industrial glass to the atomic reactor at Dounreay, the company moved into domestic glass came when George (later Lord) Mackie was appointed a director in 1966 (*Figure 10*). With glassblowers from Italy and Germany and Scottish designer Paul Ysart, Caithness Glass began making tumblers in clear and cased glass in a range of Scottish colours – peat, heather and twilight blue – some of which went particularly well with a dram of whisky.

By the 1970s, the company had branched out into copper engraved glass, led by Colin Terris, and created a bowl commissioned by the BBC for 'Mastermind' that was engraved by Denis Mann. Royal patronage came later, in the form of a Royal Warrant given by the Queen Mother. Ysart had produced glass paperweights in his spare time which inspired Terris to produce them commercially from 1970. These in turn inspired a range of jewellery in which tubes of coloured glass, drawn out rather like the strands of colour in a stick of rock, were used for the main decoration. Drawing on international success, Caithness Glass expanded in the late 1970s to open a new factory and showroom in Perth where new ranges of Art Nouveau glassware and Glenisla art ware were showcased. However, like many craft-based companies, Caithness Glass did not withstand the downturn of the 1980s and in 2002 went into receivership, now existing only as a small outlet (Carr, 1971)[2]

Another example of the theme of patronage with the intent of bringing employment to isolated parts of Scotland is Highland Stoneware, set up in Ullapool in 1974. The idea of a factory in the Scottish Highlands to make stoneware by reduction firing had been the dream (and postgraduate project) of David Grant when he went to study at the Royal College of Art in London. There the Marquess of Queensberry, then head of the department of ceramics and glass, and Grant's tutor, Grahame Clarke, so believed in Grant that they both invested in Highland Stoneware and became directors.

By the early 1980s, the company was becoming well-known for its tableware, platters, mugs, jugs, dishes and tiles (*Figure 11*). The pieces maintain a particular character because Highland Stoneware makes its own clay, glazes and decorative colours, and uses motifs of Scottish birds, animals, landscapes and seascapes. In the early days, the company was greatly helped by the support of other ceramists such as Hans Coper and Lucie Rie (and Donald Logie in Dundee), potteries such as Midwinter, Hornsea and Rosenthal, and Heals' retail outlet in London which market-tested early designs. Artists such as Eduardo Paolozzi added their own decoration to the company's ware and the Prince of Wales painted a jug with his fleur-de-lys when he visited in 1979. Twenty years later, the Prince wrote the foreword to the book celebrating Highland Stoneware's 25th anniversary (Haslam, 1999).

Figure 10. Caithness Glass. © Richard Carr Archives. Every effort has been made to identify the copyright holder. If anyone claiming copyright to this image contacts the editors with details, a full acknowledgement will appear (www.futurecraft.dundee.ac.uk) This image comes from Carr's own archive – photograph taken from press material from the 1980s. Printed with permission from Caithness Glass.

Figure 11. Highland Stoneware, Homecoming mug and plate, 2009.
Image courtesy of Highland Stoneware.

Ecclesiastical Patronage

Royal and ecclesiastical patronages have historically always had great importance to the crafts in Scotland and elsewhere, particularly with regard to stained glass and embroidery. Supported by courses at Scottish art colleges, there are strong examples of post-war stained glass in churches across Scotland. Notable work has been done by Sax Shaw, Crear McCartney (who was responsible for the window in St Magnus Cathedral, Kirkwall, Orkney which marks its 850th anniversary) and John Clark. Also notable is Douglas Hogg who, together with students at Edinburgh College of Art, was responsible for the stained glass window put into the Royal Scots Chapel in Werl, near Dortmund, Germany in 1986. Another craftsman patronised by the Church is Patrick Ross Smith, who uses the restoration of old windows, including those of synagogues, as a means of supporting 'more creative work' (Craftwork, 1983–88)[3].

Concerning embroidery, Hannah Frew Paterson undertook numerous commissions for the Church of Scotland, including the tripartite altar panels installed in Cardross Parish Church in 1981. Other embroiderers who have benefited from ecclesiastical patronage include Kathleen Whyte, Chrissie White and Marion Stewart. The Church has also commissioned various wood carvers. For example, in 1986 Peter Bailey made a lectern, table and 50 chairs from home grown oak for St Michael's Parish Church in Linlithgow, for which a brass cross was made by John Creed (Craftwork, 1983–88)[4].

But perhaps the most extraordinary act of ecclesiastical patronage was that given by The Kirk of St Nicholas in Aberdeen. Here, a memorial chapel to the oil industry was created, entered through a freestanding rood screen in wood designed and made by Tim Stead (*Figure 12*). He was also responsible for the lectern, communion table and 40 chairs in the chapel (*Figure 13*). The chapel also contains stained glass (*Figure 14*) (and a rug underneath the communion table) by Shona McInnes depicting Aberdeen's geographical features and its harbour, fishing and North Sea oil industries.

12

14

13

Figure 12. Tim Stead, freestanding rood screen.
The Kirk of St Nicholas, Aberdeen.
Image courtesy of Ruth Archibald.

Figure 13. Tim Stead, chairs in the chapel.
The Kirk of St Nicholas, Aberdeen.
Image courtesy of Ruth Archibald.

Figure 14. Shona McInnes, stained glass.
The Kirk of St Nicholas, Aberdeen.
Image courtesy of Ruth Archibald.

The way that payment was organised by Shell UK Exploration & Production, and the commission by The Kirk of St Nicholas in conjunction with the Church of Scotland's advisory committee on artistic matters, the Chaplaincy Trust, the Historic Buildings Council, the Scottish Development Agency (SDA) and representatives from the oil industry and Gray's School of Art, demonstrates how complicated and intricate such patronage can be. The memorial chapel was completed in 1989 (Carr, 1990).

Religious patronage was also provided by the building of the Tibetan Buddhist Centre, Kagyu Samye Ling in Eskdalemuir in the Scottish Borders towards the end of the 1980s. Peter Mannox made offering bowls in enamelled silver and parcel gilt, June Burleigh carpets in wool using hand knots and cut-pile, and Sonja Gerling earthenware pots, plates, jugs and bowls. John Chinnery's cast images of the Buddha and other gurus led to his being commissioned for cast rosettes and other intricate carvings for the House of Lords in London (Carr, 1986a).

Governmental Patronage

In 1944, the wartime government set up the Council of Industrial Design (CoID), 'to promote by all practical terms the improvement of design in all the products of British industry' (MacCarthy, 1972) and whose Scottish Committee held government responsibility for the crafts in Scotland. However, in the early days of the CoID Scottish craft appears to have been greatly under-represented, and not mentioned in their meeting minutes at all until December 1946 (when a competition for the design of clipped sheepskin rugs was held).

In 1948–49, the pace quickened with regard to the crafts in Scotland. An exhibition of Scottish architecture and crafts was held in Lerwick on Shetland and another, on Scottish textiles and textures, at Glasgow School of Art, while the Scottish Committee's Industrial Officer visited an existing craft centre in Morar (in Inverness-shire) to examine locally produced pottery, weaving and woodwork; and, on 1 April 1947, the idea of a series of Scottish craft groups was mooted. In 1956 and 1957, the Design Centres opened in London and Glasgow and the CoID gradually became more closely linked with consumer goods. In the 1960s, governmental responsibility for Scottish craft passed from the CoID to the Scottish Country Industries Development Trust (SCIDT) (Design Archives, 2010).

The potential for collaboration between Scottish crafts and the tourist industry was highlighted in 1949 by an exhibition of Swedish, Danish and Swiss souvenirs that opened at the Aitken Dott Galleries in Edinburgh before touring the country. A report on the industry prepared by Ian C Young, President of the Inverness Chamber of Commerce, noted its importance but also that, 'notwithstanding the many thousands of producers throughout the country, few if any are prepared to accept advice, nor are they prepared to work to a standard other than their own which, in the majority of cases, is low. There is also great unwillingness to specialise' (Design Archives, 2010).

The report proposed the establishment of a panel to judge souvenirs, a central sales organisation and the selection of approved retail outlets to sell souvenirs on a sale or return basis. It also called for a Scottish equivalent to the Den Permanente store in Copenhagen.

In November 1949, a craft conference was held in the City Chambers, Glasgow with the objective of highlighting the importance of craftsmanship in Scotland. As its chairman,

Mr John Noble of Ardkinglas, said, 'Scottish crafts are diminishing and ought to be increased. If craftsmanship dies out, our whole artistic and aesthetic standard is in grave danger.' What was needed was a craft centre that would provide propaganda, a library and a meeting place. But 'it would have to have the united support of all craftsmen in Scotland, setting high standards while not excluding anyone' – a contradiction in terms that would plague the Scottish Crafts Centre in the years to come (Design Archives, 2010).

Possibly the most important contribution made at the conference was that by Mrs Wendel of Haandarbejdets Fremme, Copenhagen, who described how the Danes had revolted against the domination of Scandinavian crafts by the Swedes, setting up the first Danish craft organisation in 1928 (a second one followed after World War II) that selected members, undertook research, organised exhibitions and sold crafts on commission. It was, she said, 'a process of turning ugly ducklings into swans' (Design Archives, 2010).

From these beginnings, the Scottish Craft Centre leased Acheson House in Edinburgh in 1951, chaired by Mr Noble and based on the Craft Centre of Great Britain. Aside from a small subsidy from the Board of Trade, the centre was self-supporting. Initially it had two members of staff (its Artistic Advisor was the Polish Count Jan Tarnowski), 121 craftsmen members (75 per cent of those who applied were rejected by a panel chaired by The Lady Sempill), 361 associate members, eleven corporate members and 15 who provided covenants.

The Scottish Crafts Centre also had a curious relationship with the CoID because, though the CoID had not helped to set it up, it advised the Board of Trade on the centre's grant. In 1957, the CoID offered to show Scottish crafts in the Design Centre in George Street, Glasgow – an offer that the membership turned down – and, in 1963, recommended that the centre adopt a more retail approach to its exhibitions and develop a photo library showing the work of Scottish craftspeople. Sir Gordon Russell, a former director of the CoID, also recommended moving the centre to Glasgow (Design Archives, 2010).

During the life of the Scottish Craft Centre until it closed its doors in 1991, it faced the drawback of being in a seventeenth-century courtyard mansion at the bottom of the Royal Mile. It was hidden behind a high wall and had a series of fine yet small rooms notable for their wood panelling, carved stonework and wrought ironwork. This discrete setting was eminently suitable for exhibitions of high quality, contemporary crafts. The trouble was, all of its members wanted to show their work. So, in 1981, there was a revolt that put an end to exhibitions of the very finest craftsmanship and turned the centre into a downmarket gift shop selling items of ordinary quality that were poorly displayed and paid scant attention to their architectural setting. At the same time, attempts to find more centrally placed premises in Edinburgh were unsuccessful (Inglehart, 1981; Carr, 1986b).

A step forward in the recognition of the importance of craft was taken in 1964 when Douglas Brims was commissioned by John Noble, then Director of The Dovecot in Edinburgh, and Harry Jefferson Barnes, Director of Glasgow School of Art, to investigate the future of craftspeople in Scotland. Brims, over a three year period, met hundreds of craftspeople, none of whom seemed to have any reference beyond themselves. Prior to his retirement in 1987 he had also organised exhibitions for craftspeople and forged links with Scottish art schools – particularly Gray's in Aberdeen and Glasgow School of Art – at a time when, amazingly, they were very well equipped but short of students (Carr, 1987b).

Figure 15. Craftwork, 1987.
© Richard Carr Archives

Every effort has been made to identify the copyright holder. If anyone claiming copyright to this image contacts the editors with details, a full acknowledgement will appear (www.futurecraft.dundee.ac.uk) This image comes from Carr's own archive – photograph taken from press material from the 1980s.

It appears that official bodies set up by successive Governments to look after the crafts in Scotland often have a short life span. In 1967, responsibility for the crafts north of the Highland Line was given to the newly-established Highlands and Islands Development Board (HIDB) despite the fact it had no crafts officer. South of the Line, SCIDT (which had originally been under the control of the agriculture and fisheries division of the Scottish Office) changed into the Small Industries Council for the Rural Areas of Scotland (SICRAS), which in turn was absorbed by the SDA when that was set up in 1977.

Governmental patronage of the crafts reached its peak during the 1980s. As the SDA's craft manager, Sally Smith led the development of the SDA's directory of craft products and its visitor guide. She also developed mail order sales to Scots living abroad, encouraged links with Scotland's tourist boards and improved the way in which crafts were supported by the country's educational system. Echoing the policy adopted by the Scottish Craft Centre by encouraging 'second tier' crafts (those that were not allied to fine art or sold by specialist galleries), she opened the SDA's own craft shop in the new Scottish Exhibition Centre in Glasgow (Smith, 2009).

Promotion of the crafts was also improved by turning the newspaper Craftwork, which had been founded in 1960, into a glossy magazine. Sadly, though beautifully written and illustrated, circulation during its five years (1983–88) only reached 2000, with barely more than 200 craftspeople buying the magazine (*Figure 15*). At the end, Craftwork's subsidy was over £4 per copy (Craftwork, 1988).

North of the Highland Line, the SDA's most significant contribution to the crafts came with the setting up of Highland Craftpoint in Beauly in 1979. It was officially opened in 1981. This was a training and research establishment that owed its inspiration to the very successful Kilkenny Workshops in Eire. Despite its somewhat remote location, in the beginning Highland Craftpoint ran a number of craft workshops and courses that were led by eminent practitioners from both sides of the Scottish Border. Sadly within a few years, Highland Craftpoint had lost its training and research roles, changed its name to Craftpoint and become an organisation solely devoted to marketing (Carr, 1985).

The SDA, in association with the Crafts Consultative Council, began a collection of Scottish crafts in 1980 that continues to grow to this day. Originally given annual funding of £8000, with a further £3000 for the HIDB, among its early acquisitions were tapestries by Archie Brennan and Fiona Mathieson, glass by Alison Kinnaird, David Cohen and David Kaplan, silverware by John Creed and metalwork by Denys Mitchell, apples and boxes in wood by Bill Childe and

Peter Roy respectively, ceramics by Mick Brettle and Iain Nelson, and textiles by Karen Alliston. It was a strong start to the collection, which remains an important source of government patronage (Craftwork, 1983–88) [5].

Public Sector Patronage

Patronage from the public sector is difficult to describe and assess because of its enormous variety and consequently this aspect of the chapter is restricted to examining the work done by particular craftspeople and the institutions involved.

Robert Stewart was arguably one of the most productive, versatile and imaginative artists/craftspeople/designers working in Scotland since World War II, spending most of his active life at Glasgow School of Art. He designed the 'Genesis' and 'Glescau' tapestries woven by The Dovecot in 1970 and 1982 for the University of Strathclyde and the City Chambers, Glasgow respectively, in addition to a tapestry for Glasgow Cathedral. Stewart was also responsible for ceramic murals beginning (in Scotland) with the Greenock Underpass in 1964–65 and including murals in West Dunbarton Burgh Offices in 1965 and the departure lounge, Prestwick Airport (1973). Altogether, Stewart completed some 20 projects, including one for Richard Attenborough's house on the Isle of Bute (Arthur, 2003).

Tim Stead was an artist/craftsman in wood who constantly blurred the boundaries between sculpture and the utilitarian object. In addition to the patronage from The Kirk of St Nicholas (previously mentioned in Ecclesiastical Patronage), Stead was privately commissioned to design and make the Papal Chair used by Pope John Paul II when he celebrated mass at Murrayfield Stadium, Edinburgh in July 1982. In the public sector, Stead often undertook relatively small commissions, including doors for the Central Govan Housing Association in Glasgow (1980) and for the Loreburn Housing Association in Dumfries (1985).

One of his most stunning creations was the wooden replica of a house in Skara Brae (the neolithic stone settlement on Orkney) in a lift shaft in the McLellan Galleries in Glasgow for the 'Scotland Creates' exhibition in 1990. He also designed 'Peephole' for the Gallery of Modern Art in Glasgow and the doorway to the education department in the National Museum of Scotland[6] in Edinburgh (both 1996). In 1999, Tim Stead and Eoin Cox set up Woodschool in Ancrum, a foundation in wood craft thus making Stead himself a patron of Scottish craftsmanship, greatly admired by the Prince of Wales. In death, Royal patronage was extended to the memory of Stead when the Prince of Wales wrote the foreword to *With the Grain*, the book celebrating Stead's life by Giles Sutherland (2005).

The role of publicly-owned art galleries and museums as patrons of the crafts has always been important since World War II. Exhibitions such as 'Jewellery Moves' and 'North Lands Creative Glass', held at the National Museum of Scotland in Edinburgh in 1998 and 2006 respectively, and the 'Face of Craft' held at the National Portrait Gallery in Edinburgh in 2006, have greatly helped to present different aspects of the crafts to the public. Kelvingrove Art Gallery and Museum regularly hosted craft fairs in the early 1980s while various galleries have practised active patronage through the purchase of craft pieces.

Patronage from galleries and museums can also take the form of commissions. In 1981, for example, Kelvingrove Art Gallery and Museum commissioned a large, glass plate from Alison Geissler and in 1986, the National Museum of Scotland invited craftspeople in Scotland to submit designs for conference tables and chairs for the Boardroom, designed and made in ash by John Makepeace at Parnham in Dorset (Carr, 1988c).

In Dundee, the McManus Galleries was patron to David Hodge and Norman Cherry in the making of a silver rose bowl and a set of silver candle holders and snuffers to commemorate the centenary of the city's museums and art galleries department in 1973. In 1991, the Roman Catholic Bishop of Dunkeld provided the funds for a silver salver, designed by Philip Chaplain and made by Kevin Allen, to commemorate Dundee's 800th anniversary (Young, 2009).

Institutional patronage takes many forms. For example in 1987, Jon Hunt designed and made a silver liqueur decanter and 20 noggins for the Incorporation of Goldsmiths in Edinburgh to give to their sister organisation in Dublin. Much larger scaled examples of institutional patronage could be Fyvie Castle in Banff and Buchan and the Mary, Queen of Scots' House in Jedburgh. The National Trust began the £600,000 restoration of Fyvie Castle in 1984, which utilised many different kinds of craftspeople including blacksmiths and upholsterers ‹http://www.nts.org.uk/›. Using craftspeople such as Denys Mitchell (metalwork), Derek Irwin (woodwork), and Liz Rowley and Anita Pate (stained and engraved glass), the reinterpretation of the Mary, Queen of Scots' House was completed in 1987 to mark the 400th anniversary of her death (Jooste, 1998).

Closing Comment

Throughout history there have been periods of uncertainty for patronage of the crafts – for example, during war, civil unrest, famine, plague and economic distress. At the time of writing, patronage of the crafts in Scotland is facing a new period of uncertainty related to restructuring and economic instability (from a global and national perspective due to the international financial collapse of 2007–2008). In terms of restructuring at the Scottish Government level, responsibility for the crafts is passing from the Scottish Arts Council (SAC) to a new body, Creative Scotland, and how things evolve and transform remains unknown. However, what is known in 2010 is that 'Craftscotland'[7] has been tasked by SAC with developing audiences through new ways of promoting and marketing craft. Led by its new Chief Executive Emma Walker, 'Craftscotland' is arguably a new dedicated form of contemporary patronage – a mixture of public sector partnerships (for example, Craftscotland and the University of Dundee through their Craft Festival Scotland initiative, 2010) and also, public and private partnerships (for example, Craftscotland and The C Word campaign where they worked with the media industry, including Onward Films and Vox Populus).

Acknowledgements

The author would like to express grateful thanks to: Ms Sally Smith, Ms Clara Young, Ms Amanda Game, Mr David Weir, Mr Ben Dawson, Dr Helen Bennett and the staff of the Design Archive, University of Brighton.

Notes

[1] Timex came to Dundee in the late 1940s. On 28 August 1993 the factory shut after six months of industrial unrest and after 47 years of presence in the City. It employed over 5000 people in the 1970s.

[2] Caithness Glass is now a division of Dartington Crystal (Torrington) Ltd.

[3] See issues of Craftwork 1983–88.

[4] ibid.

[5] ibid.

[6] When it was founded in 1861, the museum was known as the Royal Museum of Scotland and remained so until the new addition was completed at the end of the last century. It was a direct result of the Great Exhibition of 1851 and the main hall, designed by Captain Fowke of the Royal Engineers, was based upon Paxton's design of the Crystal Palace. It is now the National Museum of Scotland under National Museums Scotland.

[7] Craftscotland is a new supporting body established by SAC in 2006. For further information about Craftscotland, see http://www.craftscotland.org [Accessed March 2010].

Further Reading

Anon (1988) Craftwork: a statement from the SDA. *Craftwork*, 21, Autumn.

Arthur, L. (2003) *Robert Stewart Design 1946–95*. London, The Glasgow School of Art Press in association with A&C Black.

Bute Fabrics. (2010). [Online] Available from: http://www.butefabrics.com [Accessed February 2010].

Carr, R. (1971) Beating the Scandinavians at their Own Game. *The Guardian*, 2 September.

Carr, R. (1985) The Great Divide. *Craftwork*, 10, Winter.

Carr, R. (1986a) Eskdalemuir: The Link with Tibet. *Craftwork*, 12, Summer.

Carr, R. (1986b) The Scottish Craft Centre: A Need for Change. *Craftwork*, 11, Spring.

Carr, R. (1987a) Bute Fabrics: Marketing Design. *Craftwork*, 15, Spring.

Carr, R. (1987b) Profile: Douglas Brims. *Craftwork*, 17, Autumn.

Carr, R. (1988a) Behind the Façade. *Building Design*, 13 May.

Carr, R. (1988b) Design Policy: the RIBA award-winning General Accident HQ outside Perth. *Building Design*, 11 March 1988.

Carr, R. (1988c) Wasted Space in Edinburgh... *Design Week*, 18 March.

Carr, R. (1990) Kirk Commissions. *Crafts*, 106 September/October.

Carr, R. (1998a) Bute's Tweedy Image Takes a Back Seat. *The Scotsman*, 2 May.

Carr, R. (1998b) Look of Revelation. *Building Design*, 6 March.

Carr, R. (1998c) Look what Winning the Lottery can do to your Local Church Hall. *The Scotsman*, 23 January

Carr, R. (2008) The Colourful and Varied Tapestry that is the Dovecot, *ArtWork*, AW/25 Summer.

Craftscotland. (2009). [Online]. Available from http://www.craftscotland.org/Scottish_Parliament_Craft.htm [Accessed September 2009].

Dawson, B. (2010). [Online] Available from http://www.bendawson.com [Accessed 9 April 2010].

Dawson, B. Designer and manufacturer of furniture for architectural interiors. (Personal communication, 17 February 2010).

Design Archives, University of Brighton. (2010) [Online]. Available from: http://arts.brighton.ac.uk/collections/design-archives/ [Accessed 19 April 2010].

Haslam, M. (1999) *Highland Stoneware: The First 25 Years of a Scottish Pottery*. Somerset, Richard Dennis.

Inglehart, E. (1981) The Way Ahead for the Craft Centre. *Craftwork*, July/August.

Jooste, P. (1998) The World of Mary, Queen of Scots. [Online] Available from: http://www.marie-stuart.co.uk/Castles/MaryHouse.htm [Accessed February 2010].

MacCarthy, F. (1972) *All Things Bright & Beautiful: Design in Britain 1830 to Today*. London: George Allen & Unwin Ltd.

Smith, S. (Personal communication, 15 January 2009; 29 January 2009).

Sutherland, G. (ed.) (2005) With the Grain: An Appreciation of Tim Stead. Edinburgh: Birlinn Ltd.

The National Trust for Scotland. (2010). [Online] Available from: http://www.nts.org.uk [Accessed February 2010].

Young, Clara. Former Keeper of Decorative Art, McManus Museum & Galleries, Dundee. (Personal communication, 30 July 2009).

Past and Present Craft Practice: a frame of reference for mindful inquiry research and future craft

Louise Valentine

Introduction

In order to understand the wider context of contemporary craft and the implications of context for the future, a historical understanding is required. As Paul Greenhalgh (2007) insightfully notes,

> history provides the CV of a discipline, it records and orders its past, it allocates its
> significance to the various parts in it. In life, of course, without a good CV you don't get
> a job and without a job, you are economically crippled. In the same way, the seriousness with
> which a discipline is regarded flows heavily from how it's been dealt with historically.

This paper with its historical perspective is situated within a larger study about craft practice using the methodology *Mindful Inquiry*[1].

The historical discussion or backdrop to the critique of contemporary craft practice can be linked to the hermeneutic viewpoint of *Mindful Inquiry* as an essential level of interpretation, giving us understanding of how the past influences our present thinking. As Bentz and Shapiro (1998: 107) posit,

> modern hermeneutics argues that we cannot ever transcend our historical position,
> our viewpoint; therefore, the prejudgements that we bring to our understanding are largely
> culturally predetermined.

Historical understanding can also be linked to the role of critical social theory within *Mindful Inquiry* and in this craft research the role of critical social science is to support examination of the cultural, economic and political aspects of history in relation to the development of craft. It is to understand how craft as a discipline can support and develop communication of its value and meaning in contemporary society.

The key thinkers within two (although arguably three) aesthetic movements (Arts and Craft, and modernism including postmodernism) from the nineteenth century to the present day are used to trace the development of craft and its progress as an intellectual pursuit. The intention is to provide insight into the relation between culture, politics, society and technology within different periods and, in doing so, to facilitate a developed understanding of the values and meaning of craft. A 'pecha kucha' approach to communicating craft history (1850–2005) is used in the first part of the paper in order to pave the way for a critical review of the most recent writing about contemporary debates surrounding craft practice (2005–2010). This is also because the paper is by no means an attempt to provide a comprehensive, detailed account of craft and design history[2], for that is not the role of critical social theory or hermeneutic analysis in a *Mindful Inquiry* of craft, for which this research is a part.

A 'Pecha Kucha' of Craft History: 1850–2005

This historical frame of reference for craft practice begins with the nineteenth-century craftsman, William Morris (1834–96), as he is arguably the founder of the modern or popular notion of Arts and Crafts, with the Bauhaus, School of Ulm and modernism taking craft forward in the twentieth century.

> *The Arts and Crafts movement began with the object of making useful things, of making them well and of making them beautiful; goodness and beauty were to the leaders of the movement synonymous terms. (Ashbee, 1977: 5)*

William Morris saw this ethos as a way of bringing humanity back into the workplace and for individual workmen to have a creative input into their lives. The crucial thing about Morris was that he believed craftsmanship was the antidote to factory labour. He believed design should be inspired by nature, thus abandoning historicism, the use of trompe l'oeil (very popular at the time of the Great Exhibition, 1851) and the use of three-dimensional imaging on flat surfaces such as wallpaper and textiles. While depicted 'as a sentimental moralist' his profound vision and deep knowledge of nature and the landscape dispels this portrayal (MacCarthy, 1994). The aesthetic of William Morris' craft was as pervasive as his ethos. It was new. His aesthetic was one of material and form, of nature and natural line rather than one of illusion and historical narrative.

Moving the historical frame of reference (for interpretation of twenty-first-century craft practice) from the Arts and Craft movement to modernism is where the discussion now goes. The intention of modernism was to design a new world. Paul Greenhalgh (1990: 2–3) notes,

> *the Modern movement in design; it had two phases. The first I will fashion the phase the Pioneer phase, this opening amid the deafening thunder of the First World War and the closing with the demise of the key movements between 1929 and 1933. The second [phase which opened, in the early 1930s and closed at the end of the 1970s], I will label the International Style ... Ideologically the movement cannot be described so easily but we can say that the first phase was essentially a set of ideas, a vision of how the designed world could transform human consciousness and improve material conditions. ...The second phase was less of an idea than a style and a technology; a discourse concerned principally with the appearance of things and with their manufacture. It was expressed far more widely than the first phase.*

The first phase of modernism is epitomised through the Bauhaus, a school of thinking developed by a group of creative individuals in Germany immediately after World War I[3]. Initiated by Walter Gropius, the Bauhaus (1919–1933) school of architecture, art, design and craftsmanship was 'a unique event in cultural history' in terms of its pedagogic model, as Ludwig Grote (1968: 9) drawing on Oskar Schlemmer notes,

> *If we want to examine the essence of the Bauhaus, and determine what distinguishes it from other academies and art schools to find the basis on which rests its reputation, a diary entry by Oskar Schlemmer will provide the pertinent clue: 'the actual structure of the Bauhaus finds expression in its leader and is not restricted to any dogma, with an awareness of all that is new and topical in the world and with good motives for assimilating it. With these good motives for stabilizing it all, comes the reduction to a common denominator, the creating of a code. Hence the battle of minds, in the open or in secret, as perhaps nowhere else, a constant unrest, compelling the individual almost daily to take a stand on profound problems.' (Oskar Schlemmer, briefe und tagebucher, Munich, 1958, p 147) The open form which Gropius gave to the Bauhaus*

was the natural consequence of the open mindedness with which he approached everything new. Life was to flow freely through it, it was to be intimately related to time and its problems and not become the victim of schematism. Whenever new creative challenges presented themselves, the Bauhaus embraced them – provided they were within the realms of the possible.

Instead of following Morris' belief that craftsmanship could replace the machine, the Bauhaus believed that concepts could be developed and refined by craftsmen before being turned into a mass-produced object.

In the context of the crafts, the Bauhaus gave them a very modern form, emphasising shape, material and texture and eliminating extraneous decoration. The Bauhaus rejected historicism and encouraged pure forms that were based on geometry. Its legacy resides in its experimental approach based on examination of form and function, colour and texture and in the application of new materials such as in light fittings that were designed at the Dessau Bauhaus before being put into production by German companies at the end of the 1920s.

Despite its short history, the Bauhaus was regarded as a pedagogic success, a radical approach and liberal model for arts education that continues to exist in international art and design education (albeit to a lesser extent these days). It was one of two of the most prominent examples of educational institutes that exerted great influence on the progress of craft and design in the twentieth century. The second example was Hochschule für Gestaltung Ulm (or High School for Design). Ulm was established in post World War II Germany (1955) as a means of developing the concept of modern design, which was perceived by society as a symbol of freedom (Sparke, 1998). Ulm initially operated under the ethos of the Bauhaus, however, as time and technology progressed, so did its values and educational perspective. The intuitive model moved to a systematic one, a derivative of science and technology, with its nature being predominantly logical. This 'shift' in approach to 'rational problem-solving' adopted by Ulm caused a division within the group, between, for example, Tomás Maldonado and Max Bill. Coupled with political unease regarding Ulm's radical nature and financial problems, Ulm closed in 1968.

The influence of the Bauhaus came as the modern movement spread across Europe, following the migration of Bauhaus teachers at the end of the 1930s to the United States of America (Kardon, 1995). The outbreak of World War II (1939), among other things put a hold on the modern design movement until after 1945 when war ended.

Many of the countries that set out to reconstruct themselves after World War II wanted to project a new image of themselves in the international marketplace, and design was one of the ways they could do this.

In Europe this was most visible in the Scandinavian countries, Italy, Germany and Great Britain. Outside Europe the United States and Japan also used modern design as a showcase for their progressive economies and cultures. That of the United States was represented by the streamlined goods that were exported to many countries around the globe. In response many European countries harnessed their own traditions in an effort to differentiate themselves. Sweden and Denmark, for instance, reformulated their craft traditions in the light of requirements of modernity as a means of creating their own identity, while Italy looked to its heritage of quality and good taste to create its marketable image. (Sparke, 1998: 136)

The establishment of Cranbrook Academy of the Arts in the 1930s (Votalato, 1998), and the innovative work and ethos of American designers Charles and Ray Eames are also exemplar of this movement. Their inventive propensity, collaborative partnerships with a spectrum of industries, and their experimental ways with new material and technology shaped twentieth-century design (Albrecht, 1997).

The style of post World War II organic modernism was evident in for instance, the Eames' work and Arne Jacobsen, and this aesthetic demonstrated a shift away from the machine aesthetic toward a softer, fluid and more abstract form of visual language inspired by nature and the human body. Synthetic materials came to the fore within design and offered a bewildering range and variety of type, plastics for instance.

> The lightness, flexibility and ease of manipulation common to many of the new materials enabled designers to raise the performance capabilities of products. Advanced aluminium alloys, lightweight moly steel-tube frames and the conception of monocoque technique enabled aeronautical designers to realize the full potential of streamlining in design...Expressive use of laminated plywood for lightweight and space saving furniture was pioneered in the designs of Charles and Ray Eames ... [who] also made use of the off-the-peg industrial components including steel framing members, light weight lattice beams, metal-framed windows and high performance cladding panels, demonstrating the economy and elegance which could be achieved through the artful use of standard components. (Votalato, 1998: 135–6)

The impact of new materials was not the only contributor to a change in the economy of and for craft. The economic necessity resulting from the Great Depression had a large and direct impact on craft, as the climate forced a shift from the handmade towards industrial design and mass-manufacture. Unique objects simply became too costly to produce and purchase. The result being that a change in process, product and ideology of craft occurred[4], it was 'irrevocably altered' (Kardon, 1995: 31).

The strong American and Germanic phases of modernism were tempered by other national approaches, with Scandinavia among them making a big impact on the international marketplace, for example, the ceramic and glass craft of Kaj Franck and Tapio Wirkkala (Sparke, 1998). In the UK the work of Robin and Lucienne Day contributed to the development of craft. But, perhaps the most important aspect of the 1950s period of modernism in relation to craft was not the material and technological progress but the rise of consumption.

Consumerism was propelled forward by the youth culture of the 1960s and the

> accompanying emphasis on fun and expendability played a key role in helping to undermine the value system based on the ideas of rationality and universality, that had underpinned the Modern Movement in architecture and design. The new 'Pop' aesthetic prioritized the throw-away and the temporary and outlawed the permanent. This shift in consumption values had enormous impact (Sparke, 1998: 192).

In the 1960s and 1970s the rise of Progressivism continued and a structural shift in culture and education occurred. In particular, this period marked a distinct move away from the ideology of the Arts and Crafts movement, offering a multitude of aesthetic ideals, 'ideals that meant different perspectives on what could be deemed beautiful' (Veiteberg, 2005: 52). The purpose of objects moved from utility to lifestyle accompaniments or fashion statements. Models of craft based education prior to the 1970s were seen as vocational. However, at this time universities began to offer courses in art and/or craft where students were not so much formally taught, as encouraged to go and discover which skills they needed to create what they were working on (Adamson, 2007). The other notable educational shift in relation to the development of craft was the emergence of design method theories, through the work of, for example, Bruce Archer and John Chris Jones.

Through this shift, 'modernism' collapsed and the concept of 'postmodernism' began. In the 1980s, a commercial culture dominated postmodern design with the approach to design emphasising a 'consumer focus' rather than the modernist 'production'-led design where material and technology prevailed (Sparke, 1998).

Postmodernism in craft during the 1970s, 1980s and 1990s is epitomised through the work of, for example, woven textile engineer Junichi Arai and glass artist Dale Chihuly, (with their approach and visual signature continuing to influence the present day)[5]. Junichi Arai's respect for a meaningful relationship between the past, present and the future (in terms of skills, knowledge and culture) within the creation of new textiles underpins his design ethos, where alchemy between different forms and generations of knowledge lead his thinking. His textiles shifted attention towards the exploration of non-traditional finishing techniques, the use of natural fibres with synthetic fibres, often using synthetic materials not previously associated with textiles. The work marked a move away from traditional notions of colour, construction and finish. Dale Chihuly's large installation work of the 1970s 'far exceeded the traditional limitations of craft activities' with his bold use of colour and form and his 'ambitious approaches to crafts ... [requiring] collaboration and teamwork [where] glass-blowers [work] under the direction of Dale' (Votalato, 1998: 152 and 173, respectively). He directed the production of his ideas but did not always physically make the pieces, offering a distinctly different model for studio craft where the maker conceived the idea and through the skill of his/her hands created the physical piece.

In the 1990s diversity began to prevail within craft practice and 'the content of the term craft [became] elastic and open-ended' (Veiteberg, 2005: 40). The Netherlands and Norway in particular, arguably offered the most palpable examples of change and diversity. For example, the Dutch design group 'Droog' offered a novel 'no-nonsense' attitude towards creating highly conceptual designs with a distinct dry wit or humorous aesthetic, rather than an aesthetic emphasising style and form. Designer Hella Jongerius (through her company 'Jongeriuslab'), developed a way of working that fuses industry and craft, high and low technology, tradition and the contemporary. The wearable art of Sigurd Bronger continued to challenge the viewer to question how and if his 'jewellery' could be worn and used.

In the UK the significant shift in the culture of craft was arguably the introduction of PhD studies where a small but rising number of research degrees registered within craft disciplines, including textiles, ceramics, jewellery and glass began in the early 1990s. This rising number reflected increasing funding opportunities for such research, and the pressures on UK art schools to develop a 'research culture'. Furthermore, those craft practitioners that teach on craft design degree courses were and continue to be encouraged to shift their own work from 'professional practice' to craft practice that addresses a clearly articulated research agenda.

The rise of craft research was accompanied by the growing exploration and definition of 'practice-based' research methodologies in art and design, which seek to demonstrate the value of making as a valid methodology in its own right, and aim to redefine the nature of creative practice. Selected examples include the recycled glass research project conducted at Sheffield Hallam University under the direction of Professor James Roddis – an exemplary project on how craft research can define a research agenda and develop new insights and applications that have more widespread environmental and commercial value; Graham Whiteley whose PhD (entitled 'An Articulated Skeletal Analogy of the Human Upper-Limb') undertook prosthetic design research through a methodology that made considerable use of craft techniques such as physical prototyping and drawing, culminating in a design that was used on a 2005 Space Shuttle mission; Jayne Wallace, a jeweller, focused on exploring the potential of digital jewellery and personal experience and human relationships. Her research included making pieces that invoke the human-relational richness of jewellery to resist our expectations of the digital in order to offer fresh aesthetics and potentialities. Sandra Wilson, another jeweller and full-time tutor, focused her doctoral research on the relationship between craft and science through the application of practice-based methods.

The most striking attribute arising from this contemporary arena is the rise of new hybrid and digital forms of, and concepts for craft practice. Hybridisation of disciplines, ideas or methods offers a new intellectual space within which to explore. It presents a means to resist and experiment with traditional boundaries and perceptions of the self (as maker) and craft (as knowledge, meaning and form). This intellectual arena or '*Third Space*', notes Jorunn Veiteberg (drawing on Homi K Bhabha),

> *annuls the perceptions of history which constitutes it, and new structures continuously arise instead. But, of course, the new will be full of traces and impressions of the feelings and practices that have permeated the process. Thus, in the third space, ambiguous practices will be those that are typical, and it is possible for different practices to live side by side – without hierarchic ranking – simultaneously. (Veiteberg, 2005: 39)*

Hybridisation from this perspective offers a way of presenting craft without the traditional reference to art or design, and an opportunity for it to be understood, positioned and arguably accepted as a discipline in its own right. Digitisation and the associated digital tools (the other notable facilitator of change within craft practice during the 1990s and early twenty-first century) is a key tenet of hybrid craft practices although it also offers the lone practitioner alternative tools and methodologies for making. The work of product artist Geoffrey Mann, 3D metalworker Drummond Masterton and interactive jeweller, Hazel White, exemplify digital and hybrid craft. Mann's work is transdisciplinary, cutting across the areas of film, sculpture, physics, craft and design. It is concerned with the sinuous passage of time and space, and is manifest in glass and ceramics through high technologies. Masterton embraces CAD CAM technology in his creative process and challenges the boundaries of computer software programs. In doing so he has developed a fundamental change to the way makers interact with machine code. Hazel White's work explores the use of jewellery objects as interaction devices in digital media. Her work can be described as examples of a 'genotype' where clarification of the gene of an idea or concept is the focus of activity rather than the production of an object exposing a resolved design idea.

The aforementioned examples of postmodern craft practice (with their associated issues) are used to demonstrate the emergence of new forms of practice and new categorisations. Craft research indicates one future pathway for craft through the development of its distinctive methodologies and demonstration of its particular contribution to knowledge. This contribution is evidenced, not only in examples of innovative craft practice but in terms of its contribution to other disciplines such as aerospace engineering and HCI (human computer interaction). Moreover, it signifies an addition to the culture of craft and an alternative communication model. This cultural shift is pointing towards the emergence of a more assertive and research-grounded culture of craft practice.

The irony is, that despite the changes evidenced through postmodernism, craft in this first decade of the twenty-first century is most notably understood by popular culture as an individually designed and handmade product, a collection of historical objects showcased in a gallery or museum, a subject pursued by people who have a talent for 'making' things, or as a hobby preferred by individuals who have surplus time on their hands.

This low status of craft in contemporary culture is in large part because craft lacks both well-developed critical discourses and an explicit knowledge base, which is in contrast to the fine arts and the more industrially focused design disciplines. Craft is predominantly written about from a historical and theoretical perspective, often as the poor relation to art and/or design with historical commentaries and interpretations having the dominant voice. The voices of history and theory as ways of communicating craft remain relevant in the modern world, but they do not, arguably, generate or facilitate an awareness of the intellectual capacity of practice and the craft maker. It does not afford craft the position of an individual 'discipline', nor support the active contribution craft thinking can make to contemporary societal and economic challenges, irrespective of the context and material specialism. As a consequence, its potential is not fully reached or understood. This position has essentially been the driver for a number of critics to publish new writings which support this argument for a repositioning of craft.

Craft Theory

In 2007–2008, an unprecedented number of critical writings on craft were published[6]. They essentially called for craft to have its own theoretical meaning, rather than discussed in relation to art and design. A critical review of these form the focus of this next part of the paper, as they make clear what the current debates are surrounding craft.

Glenn Adamson's *Thinking Through Craft* (2007) explores historical and contemporary ideas surrounding 'craft'. His examination offers a range of historical, critical and cultural perspectives, giving insight into the instrumental space that craft occupies in contemporary art. In his book Adamson discusses, for example, craft as an altered currency in today's visual lexicon. He examines attitude between art and craft, provides a forum for 'thinking through craft' and what such thinking might entail and he considers the finished work (be it art, craft or design) as supplemental to the underlying concept. He does not seek or provide definitive answers, which in itself is a useful and much needed contribution to the field.

Adamson draws the reader's attention to many interesting observations and insights into the relation between art and craft, but for this historical discourse it is his focus on theorist David Pye, where Adamson claims that David Pye's *The Art of Workmanship* is the purest piece of writing on craft theory. (A view shared by many, indeed, one simply has to look at the academic publications in the last decade to confirm this). The deconstruction of Pye's writing is refreshing. He looks at the emerging relationship between artists and technicians in the 1960s and 1970s. In particular, the culture at the Royal College of Art (where Pye taught) and the role of the technician (through Ron Lenthall) are deconstructed. With Pye's notion that craft was merely a manual process and Christopher Frayling's claim that writing 'divorces manual skill from mental skill' (Adamson, 2007: 72) it is perhaps little wonder that there is an inferiority on behalf of craft. According to Adamson (2007: 72), in this climate the cultural aspects of crafted works were lost on Pye, as he points out with irony,

In his defining work The Art of Workmanship, Pye wrote, 'skill is not a word used in this book. It does not assist useful thought because it means something different in each different kind of work ... Like "function" you can make it mean what you please. It is a thought preventer'. That flat assertion is all the more remarkable given that Pye's book is the most compelling technical discussion of skilled work ever written.

Howard Risatti in his book, *A Theory of Craft: Function and Aesthetic Expression* (2007) addresses one of the most persistent issues in craft; that of craft's relationship to fine art. In the introduction he discusses how the process of 'intellectualising' art – from the Renaissance humanists to the present day – has no parallel to date in the craft field. He argues that this lack of an equal theoretical framework has cast craft in a negative light and it is this imbalance that Risatti addresses by providing a new formal theory of craft.

Risatti addresses the maze of craft terminology and the status of the crafted object in comparison to tools and machines, suggesting that 'practical function' is the key way to understand crafted objects. He makes a distinction between the skills employed by a maker and the objects which result by focusing on two principles: the function of a craft object; and the relationship between the object and the maker's hand. He examines the encroachment of design on the traditional field of craft and the impact of industrialisation on social attitudes to crafted objects. Finally, he challenges the debasement of craft by examining Kantian aesthetic theory and its claim that functional or purposive objects cannot be considered 'art'.

The abiding theme of the text is the notion of craft and the crafted object. Rather than seeing craft as a traditional practice which is unconcerned with the challenges posed by modern industrial production or an area of practice, which should be allowed to dissipate into 'fine art', Risatti argues for a theory grounded in craft's own distinguishing features; not a theory imported from elsewhere and adapted to fit.

The relation between art and craft appears to have dominated recent critical craft writing, with Richard Sennett's *The Craftsman* (2008) contributing to the discourse. Sennett's essay is about the desire to do a job and do a job well; it is concerned with delivering quality and he draws upon diverse facets of society to illustrate this, citing examples ranging from parenting to computer programming. He argues that the division of the hand and mind ultimately damages the mind, giving clarity to this view by using examples where technology was introduced to replace manual labour too quickly as in the use of computer-aided architecture at the expense of hand drawing and construction site visits. 'History' he notes, 'has drawn fault lines dividing practice and theory, technique and expression, craftsman and artist, maker and user; modern society suffers from this historical inheritance' (Sennett, 2008: 9).

Craft is looked at through a social lens and in doing so, offers an eclectic range of illustrations to expose craftsmen, craft and craftsmanship. In doing so, Sennett broadens the parameters of what constitutes craft, shifting it from skilled manual labour to a 'proposal about how to conduct life with skill' (Sennett, 2008: 9).

Continuing with the art craft, craft art debate, Brian Keeble's book, *On The Nature and Significance of the Crafts* (2005) presents three essays which explore the meaning of craft in today's increasingly mechanised society. It is a thought-provoking and at times obscure book detailing the writings of W R Lethaby, the founding principal of the Central School of Arts and

Crafts, master calligrapher Edward Johnston, and craft philosopher A K Coomaraswamy, all significant contributors to the craft movement. It discusses the differing and complementary historical and contemporary context of craft in relation to art, work, culture, spirituality and industrialisation.

Keeble's book and its essays are offered to illustrate how the nature of craft has adapted to fit society and culture historically, and argues that it must continue to do the same to remain relevant today. Whether it should or should not is arguably not the critical issue, rather it is in understanding when, where, how and why craft is positioned in this manner, and that it be one of a number of strategies in which to expose the relevance of craft and the craft maker to contemporary life.

The art craft discussion was also extended through Sandra Alfoldy's *Neocraft: Modernity and the Crafts* (2007), which presents 15 essays by different authors who have varying approaches to exploring craft including methodological approaches based in philosophy (Metcalf, Jönsson), anthropology (Howes, Milgram), history (Cumming, Myzelev) and feminism (Lemire). The unifying theme is 'Modernity', and Alfoldy posits that we must travel as far back as the Enlightenment in our debates, as this pivotal point located in history marks the place that separates tradition from modern. In relation to the purpose of this historical discourse concerning 'what is craft practice?' the work of Grace Cochrane is highlighted because of its extension into a geographical location not yet referred to in this chapter, namely Australia, and because of the genuine innovative work that she presents in relation to craft economies. Cochrane's essay attends to the issue of craftspeople and sustainable livelihoods, specifically those individuals who achieve a level of financial income that is considerably more than the internationally prevalent 'low paid, sole craft practitioner'. The projects Cochrane discusses put into practice Peter Dormer's model of 'distributed knowledge'. She demonstrates through gathered evidence that it is the practitioner's personal 'know-how' that empowers them to take charge of technology and technological processes. Cochrane discusses how craftspeople, business, and the public sector worked together in order to achieve better prospects for the individual and for the cultural profile of their respective countries. She dispels the seeming awkwardness between craft and industry by demonstrating through real life projects how design in Australia and New Zealand became a global phenomenon. In terms of communicating the significance of craft, Cochrane's model is arguably a symbol for the future as it makes clear the benefits of public funding bodies looking outward and having vision, alongside the determination and talent of the craft practitioners themselves.

In *Neocraft* Alfoldy argues for a new model of assessing craft but her subtle writing makes the problem within the existing model of assessment unclear, therefore even with a new model, how can we understand its relevance if articulation of the redundant aspects of the existing model does not exist? This is perhaps a harsh criticism given that the 'unspoken significance' of the book is that it poses the question and, in doing so, invites the reader to consider an important, related question concerning future craft: 'How will a new model of assessment contribute in a progressive way to craft and the economies of craft, namely its cultural, economic, philosophical, political, practical, social and technological economies?'

Summary

Many critics relish the opportunity to demonstrate their authority, choosing to either champion or chastise the new contributions to a field. Irrespective of journalistic or critical acclaim, it is important to note the year 2007–2008 was a turning point, signifying a genuine commitment and interest to representing the new value, meaning and form of craft to contemporary society, evidenced through the unusual number of critical writings concurrently published.

The key messages taken from these writings are:

- Craft is a discipline in its own right, rather than an adjunct to art and design.

- Craft is a constant variable; its meaning, purpose, aesthetic and economies are forever moving and transforming.

- A preference for presenting craft as a passive rather than active discipline has caused an imbalance in how its value and significance are communicated, with overemphasis given to the value of the 'made', and very little attention given to communicating the value of the maker and their intellectual agility and ability.

- Craft knowledge as a form of currency needs to be continually evaluated and used to nurture new contexts for craft and the craft practitioner. It is a key tenet of progressing craft as an economy.

- Material, technology and concept remain the three interrelated ingredients within craft practice, and are given meaning by placing them in context with contemporary cultural, economical, political and societal frameworks. The relationship offers understanding of craft as system thinking rather than independent evaluation of one tenet which offers insight into craft as a support for system thinking.

Closing Thoughts

Today, new technologies and interactive media have propelled all disciplines forward, including craft. 'The 'informationization' of the world is one of the most extensive and rapid technological shifts in human history' (Bentz and Shapiro, 1998: 17). Jorunn Veiteberg, in her keynote presentation at the 'New Craft–Future Voices' conference (2007) articulated the current intellectual landscape and intimated the need for change when communicating craft,

The tendency is clear: it is becoming more and more difficult to employ fixed, internal criteria for what makes craft 'craft'. Given the diversity that currently prevails with respect to the use of materials and ways of working it has become impossible to uphold a view of craft that is based on clear definitions of goals and means, or as a history characterised by uninterrupted and logical development in which new directions arise as further development of a shared legacy or tradition. Whether this situation means the end of craft, or an expansion of the concept of craft, is an important question, open for discussion.

In the last two years the environment for craft has been further agitated. Putting aside technological progress and pervasion of the computer, there are a number of cultural, economic and political shifts that have and will impact on society in the next decade of the twenty-first century (and beyond). For example, in 2008 the global financial system crashed and many of the world's leading banking institutions were bailed out by governmental loans of literally, hundreds of billions of dollars. In 2009, Barack Obama was elected as the first black American President of the United States of America. The economic 'meltdown' of 2008–2009 coupled with the rapid and continuing advance of communication technologies and changing landscape of global politics has yet to be understood in terms of an intellectual shift. But what is certain is that through these changes of circumstance and environment, new ways of working will emerge, attitudes and behaviour will change once again.

As the conditions of modern society and culture differ from the nineteenth and twentieth centuries the need for interpretation of craft in order to discover and apply its meaning in the modern context is clear. A mindful reassessment of 'what is craft practice?' is needed to expose how and why twenty-first-century craft is both different and similar to its predecessors. In conclusion, it is presented that phenomenological, heuristic and hermeneutic perspectives are required in order to achieve balance between the history, theory and practice of craft thereby understanding and communicating it as a discipline. This is the vision for future craft.

Notes

[1] I affirm that I am not a historian, nor seek to be. Indeed, for a full and rich appreciation of the history of craft and design, I urge the reader to reference the notable work of, for example, Sandra Alfoldy, Annette Carruthers, Elizabeth Cumming, Sir Christopher Frayling, Paul Greenhalgh, Tanya Harrod , Guy Julier, Catherine McDermott, Victor Margolin, Bruce Metcalf, Penny Sparke, Greg Votalato. In parallel with this, I encourage notable curators of craft to be contacted also, including, for example, Grace Cochrane, Amanda Game, Monica Gasper, Elizabeth Goring, Martina Margetts and Jorunn Veiteberg.

[2] For a thorough and complete discussion of design history, I suggest reading the work of Victor Margolin and Clive Dilnot, particularly their essays in, Margolin, V. [ed.] (1989) *Design Discourse: history, theory and criticism*. USA: the University of Chicago Press. See also the further reading section.

[3] It operated during a period of intense change in Europe, when the Russian Revolution of 1917 led to fears that it would spread throughout the Continent, while the end of the Austro-Hungarian and German empires of 1919 led to the redrawing of the map of Europe (and of other parts of the world) at the Treaty of Versailles. Germany's Weimar Republic, in particular, struggled to cope with the high levels of unemployment and hyperinflation during the 1920s, but, on the other hand, there was a belief that World War I was the war to end all wars and it marked the true end of the nineteenth century. While there was cultural turmoil resulting from World War I, it was also a time when people had great hope for the future (Scheidig, 1967; Forgacs, 1995).

[4] The vast reduction in the cost of electricity between 1920 and 1960 greatly contributed to the development of new materials, as did the positive relation between chemistry and electricity. This contributed to major improvements in manufacturing for both industrial and household-scale objects and services. Nuclear power came into focus in the late 1950s. The chemical industries flourished.

[5] It is acknowledged that there are many notable people who could have been cited as exemplars of postmodernist craft practice (including, ceramist and artist, Peter Voulkos; jewellers, Gijs Bakker and Sigurd Bronger; textile artist Caroline Broadhead). As the purpose of this paper is to highlight the change rather than discuss and debate it, it was deemed unnecessary to do so.

[6] In parallel with literary publication, there was a raising of profile and interest in international conferences and events. For example, European Conference on Craft and Small Enterprises, Stuttgart, April 2007, 'Challenges and opportunities for craft and small enterprises in the European Single Market'; 'Craft Has No Boundaries', Craft Organization Development Association (CODA) International Leadership Conference, Calgary, Canada, June 2007; 'New Craft – Future Voices', Dundee, Scotland, July 2007; 'Neocraft', Nova Scotia College of Art and Design, Canada, November 2007. The commitment of the global sector to present Craft in a new light was palpable.

Further Reading

Adamson, G. (2007) *Thinking Through Craft*. UK: Berg.

Albrecht, D. (1997) Design is a Method of Action. In: The Library of Congress in Partnership with the Vitra Design Museum. (1997) *The Work of Charles and Ray Eames: a legacy of invention*. New York: Harry M Abrams Inc.

Alfoldy, S. [ed.] (2007) *Neocraft: Modernity and the Crafts*. Canada: The Press of Nova Scotia College of Art and Design.

Alfoldy, S. and Helland, J. [eds.] (2008) *Craft, Space & Interior Design, 1855–2005*. Halifax: The Press of the Nova Scotia College of Art and Design.

Ashbee, C.R. (1977) *Craftmanship in Competitive Industry*. New York, London: Garland Publishing, Inc.

Bentz, V. M. and Shapiro, B. (1998) *Mindful Inquiry in Social Research*. Newbury Park, London, New Delhi: Sage Publications.

Briggs, A. [ed.] (1962) *William Morris: selected writings and designs*. Middlesex, England: Penguin.

Briggs, A. (1979) *Iron Bridge to Crystal Palace: impact and images of the industrial revolution*. London: Thames and Hudson Ltd.

Forgacs, E. (1995) *The Bauhaus Idea and Bauhaus Politics*. Budapest: Central European University Press.

Frayling, C. (1987) *The Royal College of Art: one hundred and fifty years of art and design*. London: Barrie & Jenkins Ltd.

Greenhalgh, P. [ed.] (1990) *Modernism in Design*. London: Reaktion Books.

Greenhalgh, P. (2007) Craft and the New Humanism. Keynote Presentation given at the International Conference, '*New Craft – Future Voices*', 4–6 July 2007, University of Dundee, Scotland.

Henderson, P. (1967) *William Morris: his life, works and friends*. London: Thames and Hudson Ltd.

Kardon, J. [ed.] (1995) *Craft in the Machine Age: the history of twentieth-century American craft 1920–1945*. New York: Harry Abrams Inc.

Keeble, B. (2005) *On the Nature and Significance of the Crafts*. London: The Temenos Academy.

MacCarthy, F. (1972) *All Things Bright & Beautiful: Design in Britain 1830 to today*. London: George Allen & Unwin Ltd.

MacCarthy, F. (1994) *William Morris: a life for our time*. London: Faber and Faber.

Margolin, V. [ed.] (1989) *Design Discourse: history, theory and criticism*. USA: the University of Chicago Press.

Risatti, H. (2007) *A Theory of Craft: Function and Aesthetic Expression*. USA: The University of North Carolina Press.

Royal Academy of Arts. (1968). *50 years Bauhaus: German Exhibition, 21 September – 27 October 1968*. London: Royal Academy of Arts.

Scheidig, W. (1967) *Weimar Crafts of the Bauhaus: 1919–1924 an early experiment in industrial design*. London: Studio Vista.

Sennett, R. (2008) *The Craftsman*. Great Britain: Allen Lane.

Sparke, P. (1998) *A Century of Design: design pioneers of the 20th century*. London: Mitchell Beazley.

Veiteberg, J. (2005) *Craft in Transition*. Bergen, Norway: Bergen National Academy of the Arts.

Votalato, G. (1998). *American Design in the Twentieth Century*. Manchester and New York: Manchester University Press.

Visual Thinking beyond Phoebe Anna Traquair's Craft Making

Fanke Peng

Introduction

Over the last decade, visual culture has become a crucial means by which social scientists understand social culture; linguists understand communication and psychologists study man's thinking. Visual culture encompasses a wide range, including painting, advertising, photography and films. Perhaps, unsurprisingly, craft has not been considered within this 'range', maybe because of Risatti's debate about visual meaning and social structure between fine art and craft – fine art entails the making of symbols, whereas craft entails the making of things (Risatti, 2007). This position reflects the difference in treatment between fine art and craft, in terms of 'visual culture'. Craft has usually been perceived as being physical, that is, actual objects, which have an applied function. In our contemporary social culture, there is the tendency to 'overestimate' craft's physical aspect (skilful making) and 'underestimate' its social aspect (visual thinking).

Craft's social aspect has led the author to explore its visual meaning; however, the existing visual approaches to visual meaning in social science are restricted in their application to art (fine art). The problem a craft researcher faces is the question of how to settle a craft object's meaning through interpretation. This quest has provided the author with opportunities to choose and test some existing visual methodologies on craft objects.

The volume of visual methods is growing ever larger and this paper is unable to cover all the genres. The author has identified an opportunity to depart from contemporary analytical approaches to visual art, such as those of history, perceptual psychology, social semiotics and craft practice, in order to develop a systematic visual analysis model (VAM) which can be used as a tool to analyse a craft object from the practitioner's perspective.

When we consider the existing analytical approaches to visual intelligence, there are many linguists, including Gunther Kress and Theo Van Leeuwen, who have studied the analysis of verbal texts and, increasingly, are applying semiotic methods to visual communication. Arnheim argued that there are 'powerful prejudices' between visual thinking and verbal analysis (*ie* the linguists' approach).

> One of these prejudices asserts that visual things cannot be expressed in words ... another prejudice maintains that verbal analysis will paralyse intuitive creation and comprehension. (Arnheim, 1954: vi)

Both prejudices have a core of truth and both can be applied to the issue of the difference between 'analysing visual image' and 'visually analysing'. The latter is the author's aim for the VAM.

Visual analysis is concerned with the mode of dynamic simultaneity, seeing as one whole event. By delving into visual analysis, we find that, 'our attention expands to experience this action as one whole that is its own present moment' (Bortoft, 1996: 64). This dynamic action – visually analysing, reawakens our inborn capacity to understand through the eyes.

This mode of visual analysis achieves, 'the potential capacity to "see" and reach the un analyzable' (Arnheim, 1954: vi). It is a holistic analysis and it is not new to the artist and craftsman that,

> *a whole cannot be attained by adding up isolated parts. In fact, something like an artistic look at reality was needed to remind scientists that most phenomena of nature are not described adequately if they are analyzed piece by piece. (Arnheim, 1954: vii)*

An analytical mode is not, thus, opposed to a holistic mode, in the same way that separate parts differ from the whole but are not opposed to it. The author intended to identify a visual analysis model, which can visually analyse and is a dynamic mode, which requires holistic seeing. This is proposed in response to the gaps identified in current visual methodologies, in particular, in an effort to help to understand the 'visual thinking'.

Before considering construction of the VAM, it was necessary for the author to contemplate holistic seeing, as this formed an integral and essential part of the model. Existing holistic ways of seeing in both West and East were considered, to allow a contextual review of the holistic modes of consciousness.

In the West, Goethe's scientific method arguably established a systematic approach to conscious participation. Goethe's methodology involves the observer as a participant and encourages understanding by acknowledging the relationship between form and process (Wahl, 2007). Goethe's conscious–process–participation epistemology, dynamic understanding of form as an expression of process and his extraordinary way of seeing a flowering plant in the process of visual analysis, gave the author an essential insight for understanding craft process through the craft object (form).

Eastern Zen philosophy has a strong parallel with Western holistic ways of seeing. It offers a way of obtaining reliable knowledge about the nature of reality. Zen's way encourages holistic seeing, with systematic thinking and process consideration. Systematic thinkers believe that the component parts of a system can best be understood in the context of their relationship with each other and with other systems, rather than in isolation. Process consideration is connected with the natural transformation in the full range, especially where the growth proceeds by metamorphosis (Bortoft, 1996). Therefore, holistic ways of seeing offer a vehicle to create a suitable holistic model for analysing craft practice.

By combining the holistic approach to the already mentioned analytical approaches in social science and fine art, our contemplation of craft practice acquires a new dimension. Having created an augmented approach to the VAM, it is then necessary to apply it to actual craft objects; to test its veracity and value.

Visually Analysing Craft Objects in the Field

In order to test the performance of this exploratory model and explore the act of visually analysing craft practice, the work of Phoebe Anna Traquair was chosen. Phoebe Anna Traquair (1852–1936) was one of the first significant arts and crafts women in modern Scotland (Cumming, 2005)[1]. The work of Phoebe Anna Traquair was selected because she was one of the leading practitioners in the Arts and Crafts movement in the late nineteenth and early twentieth centuries. The quality of her works, their availability for primary investigation, and the diversity of practice (in that different skill sets were required for different forms of practice) were additional criteria for practitioner selection. Most importantly most of her high-quality works are accessible in Scotland.

Her work has been collected by organisations such as the National Museums Scotland, the City of Edinburgh Museums and Galleries, the National Trust for Scotland and the Trustees of the National Library of Scotland. Inclusion in national collections is viewed as a testament to the quality of work she produced and a formal recognition of the contribution of her work to the visual arts.

Traquair played with scale, adopting different approaches depending on the artistic media. She produced a substantial body of work in the form of large mural decoration, life-size embroidery, bookbinding, small-scale enamelling and illuminated manuscripts.

Case study was adopted as the method for guiding the application and development of the VAM through Traquair's work. Case study is a way of investigating an empirical topic by following a set of pre-specified procedures (Yin, 2003). It is a method that offers the opportunity to explore a situation from a plurality of perspectives before making any judgements (Valentine, 2004).

In relation to testing the VAM through the work of Phoebe Anna Traquair, there was a single case study with holistic designs for three reasons: the VAM is a combination of holistic and analytical modes of consciousness, Traquair's work is unique and highly innovative and thirdly, the VAM is a newly devised model.

Data collection was another important part in the design of this case study. Yin (2003) pointed out that the approach to collecting data for case study can include documentation, archival records, interviews, direct observations, participant observation and physical artefacts. Besides studying the historical documentation, archival records and physical artefacts, the author also decided to combine interview, direct observations and participant observation to gather insightful and primary data. For example, by making a field visit to the case study 'site', the author was creating the opportunity for direct observations.

The author collected data by engaging in fieldwork, thus making direct observation of Traquair's work. She visited three buildings in which Traquair's mural decorations are housed in Edinburgh. She followed the order in which Traquair created the murals, and used the timeline to observe the progress in Traquair's craft practice (*Figure 1*). This helped the author to see and experience the visual progress in Traquair's process. Observation of two embroideries in situ was also undertaken for the study along the time sequence. The embroideries differ from the murals in terms of the environment in which they are located. While the murals are located in a fixed space (*Figure 2*), the embroideries are portable and have had many spaces. 'The Salvation of Mankind' is in a collection at the City Art Centre (City of Edinburgh Museums and Galleries). However, the author had the opportunity to see this piece in several different exhibitions during the three years of study; one example being the 'Hand, Heart and Soul' exhibition at the City Art Centre, Edinburgh, in 2007.

Within Traquair's work, the author identified that mural decoration and embroidery represent the major aspects of her craft practice. Direct observation of Traquair's work was conducted over 18 months. The mural works are housed within the Mortuary Chapel of the Royal Hospital for Sick Children, the Song School of St Mary's Episcopal Cathedral and the

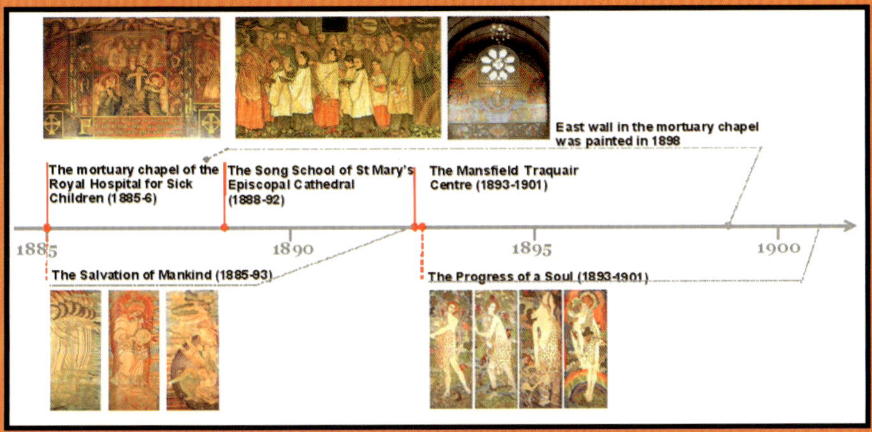

Figure 1. A timeline 1885–1902 for the creation and completion of five major works by Phoebe Anna Traquair.

Figure 2 Detailed image – Traquair's mural of the 'Wise and Foolish Virgins' in the former Catholic Apostolic Church, Edinburgh. Photograph Stewart Guthrie, © Mansfield Traquair Trust.

Mansfield Traquair Centre. The embroidery works observed were 'The Salvation of Mankind' and 'The Progress of a Soul'. Each of Traquair's mural decorations and embroideries took several years to create, for example, the mural within the Song School of St Mary's Episcopal Cathedral took five years to complete, the Mansfield Traquair Centre mural took nine years, 'The Salvation of Mankind' required nine years and 'The Progress of a Soul', nine years.

As well as observing the historical visual practice of Traquair, the researcher was observing the application of the new VAM. Therefore, the phenomenon is not purely historical, nor is it purely theoretical or practical, rather it is a combination of all three. In relation to this, there is some relevant behaviour or environmental conditions (which are available for observation) that must be acknowledged (Yin, 2003). The observations are the researcher's application of theory in practice, these serve as a central source of evidence in this study. It is also the relationship between the subject of the phenomenon (*ie* VAM), the researcher's tacit knowledge and the visual work of Traquair. As the issue of 'bias' is an important consideration when observing data (Cohen and Manion, 1980: 53), the researcher ensured it was not disturbed by adhering to the rules of engagement set by museums and exhibitions which do not allow the works to be handled by visitors. As the opportunity to talk to the practitioner was not an option (as she died in 1936), the author engaged in a 'dialogue' with the work in situ, which allowed the author to have a 'conversation' with the practitioner, where her visual thinking was driving the direction of the conversation.

In relation to testing the theory of the VAM in practice and using the historical craft practice of Phoebe Anna Traquair, both participant and non-participant approaches to observation were employed, as the dialogue between theory and practice requires this. When observing Traquair's work in situ, non-participant observation was used but when applying the VAM to Traquair's work, participant observation was employed. The theory of the VAM (three levels of observation and 13 ways of seeing) was the mechanism for ensuring the author was not overwhelmed by the complexity of Traquair's work and did not lose perspective and become blind to the peculiarities of visual thinking under investigation.

Discussion

The application of the VAM – the three levels of observation and the associated 13 ways of seeing[2] – has been explored in depth in each piece of work to analyse how the ways of seeing have influenced the way the author appreciates the craft objects and practice, and captured the spiritual force that Traquair created in her visual work. The author identified that, for certain aspects, particular ways of seeing proved to give great insight. To test the VAM, one embroidery and one mural were chosen.

The mural in the Song School of St Mary's Episcopal Cathedral was chosen because according to Cumming (2005), it represented a new stage in the development of Traquair's mural work, as opposed to earlier work in the Mortuary Chapel of the Royal Hospital for Sick Children. When a mural decoration is created, the colours will vary in accordance with the source of light, such as candlelight, daylight and electric light. In the Mortuary Chapel, originally a small, windowless coalhouse, only four by three metres in size, there was limited daylight available, while the only artificial lighting available at the time (1885) was a coal lamp. Therefore, lighting was one of Traquair's challenges in creating the mural in the Mortuary Chapel. In the Song School, Traquair had sufficient space to fully express her visual language. Furthermore, there were large windows which allowed ideal natural lighting into the interior space. This permitted the practitioner to see the mural during the day, without the aid of artificial light.

By applying the VAM in the three levels of observation and the associated 13 ways of seeing, the interactive relationship was identified as one of the most insightful ways of seeing in analysing the mural in the Song School of St Mary's Episcopal Cathedral. Figure 3 illustrates the interactive relationship between the mural and the viewer in the building.

Figure 3. A study of 'The Powers of the Lord' in the Song School and an application of the VAM, indicate the branching structure and the parallel path approach, the process of visually analysing has been manifested via interactive media tools.

A study of the mural in the school reveals the branching structure[3] and the parallel path approach[4]. The narrative elements 'inside' the murals are usually arranged and defined as branch points, which are placed along particular viewing positions 'outside' the murals. In a moving process, these particular viewing positions create the routes of the flow; the flow 'inside' the mural would be represented by the 'outside' flow (*Figure 3*). The result is parallel paths.

Figure 4 illustrates the underlying structures. The blue dots represent the figures on the mural panels, while the white dots depict the viewer's corresponding positions in the seeing process.

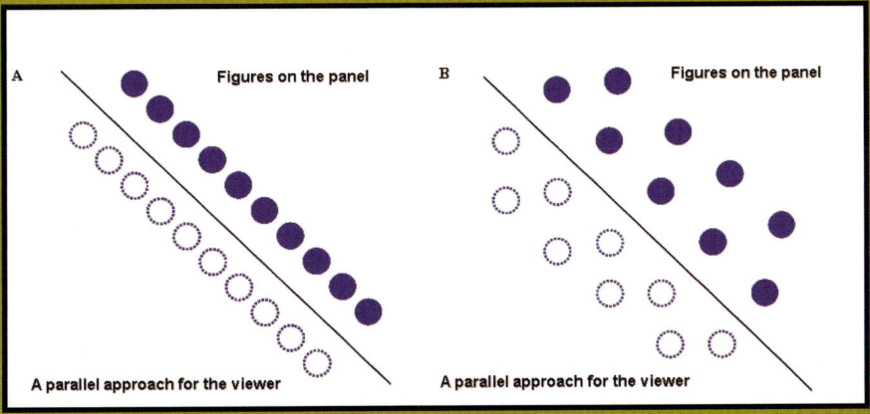

Figure 4. The parallel approach (Peng, 2010).

Figure 5. Phoebe Anna Traquair,
'The Progress of a Soul' (1893—1902),
Left to right: 'The Entrance' (1893-95),
'The Stress' (1895-97), 'Despair' (1897-99),
'The Victory' (1899-1902).
National Gallery of Scotland.

To test the VAM in Traquair's embroidery, the author chose Traquair's 'The Progress of a Soul' (*Figure 5*). The reasons for the choice of an acknowledged masterpiece are its high quality and the complexity of subject within the aesthetic composition.

By applying the VAM in the three levels of observation and the associated 13 ways of seeing, Flow and Rhythm[5] has been identified to be the most insightful way of seeing in 'The Progress of a Soul'.

The VAM suggests that rhythm helps to explain how craft practitioners create structural organisation in their work, according to how humans see form, pattern, shape or total configuration in terms of group relationships, rather than individual items. Flow and Rhythm have been used to articulate the structural organisation on each individual panel and their meaning as regards the group relationship of 'The Progress of a Soul'. There are two major concerns: flow and the driving force (the energies and the tensions in the visual images) between top and bottom, left and right across 'The Progress of a Soul'.

The VAM indicates that the driving force of the flow could be described as the use of repeated line, shape, colour, texture or pattern. In this piece, there are different flows between top and bottom; they are driven by birds at the top, harps in the middle and animals at the bottom.

The VAM identified a group of flow and rhythm in the upper space (*Figure 6*) across the four panels, which were created by birds. On the first panel, they are flying in two parallel lines to express the sense of harmony and innocence of this image. Because of the increasing tensions on the second panel, the birds are more disorderly. When the scenario turns to despair, they perch on a branch, bow their heads in sympathy with nature and the silence of despair. One bird sits further away, imitating Denys' loneliness and despair. There are fewer birds representing the loss of life. They are, however, singing once more in the last embroidery, 'The Victory', a sign of the joy and triumph of life over death.

The VAM identified a group of rhythms across the middle of the four panels, which was created by harps. The harps dominate the middle and central part of the spaces (*Figure 7*). They help to push the scenario and accompany the main body in the centre of each panel. The golden harp is highlighted in the space but does not interfere with the narrative of the main character – Denys. In the second panel, the strings of the harp are broken, to infer the vicissitudes of Denys' life and the silence of despair. These harps create flow across panels and also reflect the immensity of spiritual life and culture.

The VAM identified a group of rhythms at the lower level of the four panels, which was created by a rabbit, a large bird and a reptile. The rabbit and the reptile dominate the lower part (*Figure 8*). A rabbit dominates the central lower foreground on the first panel and left edge of the second one. The rabbit is a 'traditional symbol of lust: the panel is concerned with the pleasures of youth as much as innocence' (Cumming, 2005: 65). In the second panel, the rabbit hangs dead from the beak of a large bird, while a reptile starts to wrap itself around Denys' legs. A butterfly is positioned just beside the mouth of the reptile. The rabbit, large bird, reptile and butterfly, all emphasise the tension in the scenario of the four panels. In the third panel the reptile, which dominates the central lower foreground, is wrapped around Denys' legs; it is increasing in size and its colours present a vivid warning. The whole of this panel reflects despair, with the exception of the reptile which is a religious symbol of Satan. The fourth and final scene resolves Traquair's narrative.

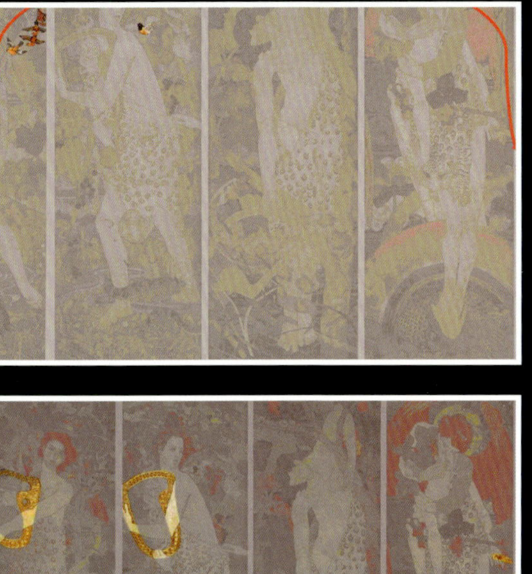

Figure 6. The sub-driving force – birds at the upper level.

Figure 7. The sub-driving force – harps in the middle.

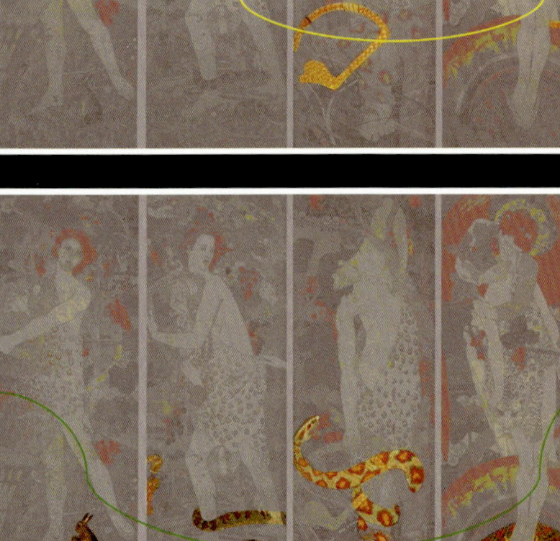

Figure 8. The sub-driving force – rabbit, large bird and reptile at the lower level.

Figure 9. The driving forces between top and bottom across the four panels.

The different sequences create different spatially driven themes on the panels (*Figure 9*). They help to maintain the readability of narration, through balanced decoration. The animation and vibrancy of the composition as a whole reflect the intensity that lies both on the surface and within the depth of the images.

'The Progress of a Soul' depicts a figure in four stages. The flows are running smoothly across the four panels, between left and right, up and down, foreground and background. This is created by simply repeating; thus, the flow and rhythm in the embroideries are dynamic (*Figure 10*). Besides the principal figure in the middle of each panel, the detailed visuals, such as harps, rabbits, butterflies, birds and reptiles, have vividly reflected the theme of the embroideries.

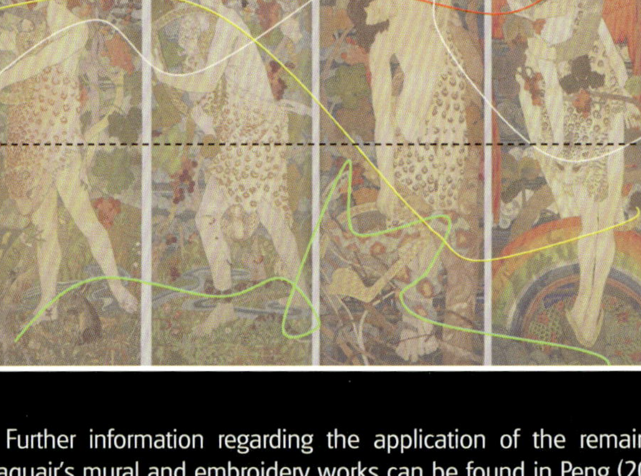

Figure 10. The dynamic movement and growth in 'The Progress of a Soul'.

Further information regarding the application of the remaining 13 ways of seeing in Traquair's mural and embroidery works can be found in Peng (2010).

Closing Comment

The case study confirmed the value of the VAM, in understanding the craft practitioner's visual thinking, by complementing existing historical and theoretical approaches to appreciating craft. Art historians have identified some of the key components of Traquair's visual work. The art historian's approach to the visual depends on what Irit Rogoff (1998: 17) calls, 'the good eyes', that is, 'a way of looking at paintings that is not methodologically explicit but which, nevertheless, produces a specific way of describing paintings' (Rose, 2001: 33).

The art historian's approach to visual culture offers ways of describing a piece of visual work in terms of content, colour, spatial organisation, light and expressive content (Rose, 2001). For example, Elizabeth Cumming's approach to Traquair's work provided much knowledge about the nature of the work of Traquair and specifically about the types of visual imagery which she considered and which inspired the work. This is very useful as a first stage in beginning to describe the visual impact of an image but it lacks methodological explicitness. It is a descriptive method, rather than an analytical model. Thus, the art historian's approach claims to look at images for 'what they are', rather than discuss the rationale behind them with regard to composition. Furthermore, the art historian's approach does not consider the differences in visual thinking between visual thinking as regards two-dimensional visual images and three-dimensional visual forms. Differing from the descriptive methods in the historian's approach to visual culture, the VAM is a practical analytical model for visually analysing the visual meaning in craft objects. The rationale behind the visual composition has thus been identified, through the application of the VAM.

The testing of the VAM in a historical context, with specific reference to the work of Phoebe Anna Traquair, focused on the analysis of two-dimensional forms of visual communication. Much was learned about the value and effectiveness of the VAM through the Phoebe Anna Traquair case study, but further applications of the VAM were required. The author then shifted the context and focus away from history towards the present day and, from two-dimensional visual imagery to three-dimensional visual form. The qualitative approach to research was maintained. The objective was to examine whether the VAM was transferable within different forms of craft practice: to explore to what degree the VAM can be applied to three-dimensional visual forms and to establish the differences, if any, between two-dimensional and three-dimensional visual craft practice.

The three-dimensional visual form was the major criterion for choosing an appropriate craft practitioner's work for analyses. The work of Michael Lloyd was chosen because of his pursuit of three-dimensional form and pattern. Michael Lloyd is a silversmith of international standing, who has been working within the field for over 30 years. His work has been exhibited and collected by many societies, galleries and museums, such as the Victoria and Albert Museum in London and the National Museums Scotland. His reputation as a quality silversmith has also brought prestigious commissions. For example, Lloyd created a national Mace in 1999, to celebrate the return of a Parliament to Scotland after 300 years; it is placed at a focal point in the debating chamber during sittings of the Scottish Parliament.

Lloyd demonstrates a high quality and visual distinctiveness in his work. His use of materials, techniques, forms and the context of the work are very different from those in the historical case of Phoebe Anna Traquair. These differences provided the springboard for testing the VAM in relation to three-dimensional contemporary craft, as opposed to two-dimensional craftwork. The work of a silversmith has different visual imperatives from those constructed in a two-dimensional field, such as murals and embroideries. Testing the VAM in this way allowed a comparison between two- and three-dimensional visual forms.

The author applied her VAM to Michael Lloyd's silversmithing work through the use of interactive media. This allowed her to modify the scale of her VAM to be able to read the language inherent within small-scaled, three-dimensional object(s). The VAM could not be transferred without modification to small 3D objects[6]. For example, when visually reading form, there are different interactive relations involved. In addition, small-scaled craft objects require different consideration, as opposed to two-dimensional visual images and large-scaled objects. Smaller objects demand an intimacy and engagement, to satisfy the viewer's physical sensory needs.

The author significantly modified the VAM to enable it to function fully as an analytical tool for the visual analysis of 3D craft. 3D objects convey their visual intention differently from 2D objects. Within a craft practitioner's visual thinking, the elements of shape and form are not purely compositional within which to hold decorative pattern, rather they are the visual language of the practitioner.

The visual analysis model will be further explored and evaluated in depth in future research, by examining how the VAM has influenced the way we read the craft object and practice and how we capture the visual meaning that craft practitioners create in their visual work. The VAM will also be further developed into an interactive tool, so that it is accessible and transferable. This would allow for it to be evaluated across the spectrum of craft objects and practices.

Notes

[1] There was complete silence about Traquair and her work during World War I. Elizabeth Cumming is the first contemporary historian to put Traquair back on the cultural map. She has set Traquair as her main research topic since her PhD in the mid-1980s. Cumming introduced Traquair to today's audience.

[2] Further information regarding the 13 ways of seeing can be found in the PhD thesis *Visual Thinking – Beyond Craft Making: identifying and verifying a visual analysis model for craft practice* (Peng, 2010 Chapter 3).

[3] In the branching structure, the plot begins at the base node and certain points in the story are defined as branch points, where the plot splits into its separate paths. With no recombination of threads, the branching structure leads to a number of end points equal to the number of branch points plus one (for two-way branching) or even more (for multi-path branching) (The International Game Developers Association, 2009).

[4] The parallel path approach (which could also be considered as a fully recombined branching structure) is a tenable and useful approach to visualising the relationship between a viewer and a series of mural panels.

[5] The flow in a visual image is made up of the variety of beats and rhythms in the work. The rhythm could be described as the usage of repeated line, shape, colour, texture or pattern.

[6] Further information regarding the modification of the VAM to small 3D objects can be found in the PhD thesis Visual Thinking – Beyond Craft Making: identifying and verifying a visual analysis model for craft practice (Peng, 2010 Chapter 5).

Further Reading

Allardyce, F., Mann, R. and Historic Scotland – Technical Conservation Research and Education Division. (2007) *Conservation of Phoebe Anna Traquair murals at Mansfield Traquair Centre Edinburgh: 1 case study.* Edinburgh, Historic Scotland.

Arnheim, R. (1954) *Art and Visual Perception: a psychology of the creative eye.* Berkeley: University of California Press.

Arnheim, R. (1970) *Visual Thinking.* London: Faber.

Baird, C. and Watban, B. (2007) *The Cutting Edge: Scotland's Contemporary Crafts.* Edinburgh: NMS Enterprises Ltd.

Berger, J., Dibb, M. and British Broadcasting Corporation (2008) *Ways of seeing: episode 1-4.* [London], BBC.

Bohm, D. (1994) *Thought as a System.* London: Routledge.

Bohm, D. (2002) *Wholeness and the Implicate Order.* London: Routledge.

Bohm, D. (2004) *On Dialogue.* London: Routledge.

Bortoft, H. (1996) *The Wholeness of Nature: Goethe's way of science.* Edinburgh: Floris Books.

Cohen, L. and Manion, L. (1980) *Research Methods in Education.* London: Croom Helm.

Cumming, E. (1986) *Phoebe Anna Traquair HRSA (1852-1936) and her contribution to arts and crafts in Edinburgh.* [electronic resource], University of Edinburgh.

Cumming, E. (1993) *Phoebe Anna Traquair.* Edinburgh: Scottish National Portrait Gallery.

Cumming, E. (2005) *Phoebe Anna Traquair: 1852–1936.* Edinburgh: National Galleries of Scotland in association with the National Museums of Scotland.

Cumming, E. (2006) *Hand, Heart and Soul: the Arts and Crafts movement in Scotland.* Edinburgh: Birlinn.

Cumming, E. and Kaplan, W. (1991) *The Arts and Crafts Movement.* London/New York: Thames & Hudson.

Danto, A. C. (1986) *The Philosophical Disenfranchisement of art.* New York: Columbia University Press.

Dewey, J. (1958) *Art as Experience.* New York: Capricorn Books.

Hoffman, D. D. (1998) *Visual Intelligence: how we create what we see.* New York: Norton.

Kress, G. R. and Van Leeuwen, T. (1996) *Reading Images: the grammar of visual design.* London, New York: Routledge.

Krishnamurti, J., Bohm, D. and Shainberg, D. (1978) *The Wholeness of Life.* London: Gollancz.

Lane, P. (1998) *Ceramic Form: design & decoration.* New York: Rizzoli International Publications.

Naisbitt, J. (2006) *Mind Set: reset your thinking and see the future.* New York, Collins.

Peng, F. (2010) *Visual Thinking − Beyond Craft Making: identifying and verifying a visual analysis model for craft practice.* [Dundee], [University of Dundee].

Risatti, H. (2007) A Theory of Craft: function and aesthetic expression, Chapel Hill, University of North Carolina Press.

Rose, G. (2001) *Visual Methodologies: an introduction to the interpretation of visual materials.* Thousand Oaks, Calif.; London: SAGE.

Scottish National Portrait Gallery (Edinburgh) and Cumming, E. (1993) *Phoebe Anna Traquair* [catalogue of the exhibition held at the Scottish National Portrait Gallery, 6 August−7 November 1993], National Galleries of Scotland.

Sherman, D. J. E. and Rogoff, I. E. (1998) Museum Culture: histories, discourses, spectacles: Conference entitled 'The institutions of culture: the museum': Papers, Routledge.

Valentine, L. (2004) *The Activity of Rhetoric within the Process of a Designer's Thinking.* [Unpublished Doctoral Thesis]. University of Dundee, Scotland.

Wahl, D. (2007) 'Scale-linking Design for Systemic Health: Sustainable Communities and Cities in Context', *International Journal of Ecodynamics,* Vol.2 No.1, pp.57-72

Wilson, S. (2005) *The Organics of Craft: the influence of Goethe's holism.* [Unpublished Doctoral Thesis]. University of Dundee, Scotland.

Yanagi, S. E. and Leach, B. (1989) *The Unknown Craftsman: a Japanese insight into beauty.* Tokyo/London: Kodansha International.

Yin, R. K. (2003) Case Study Research: design and methods. Thousand Oaks, Calif.; London: SAGE.

Craft and the New Humanism
Paul Greenhalgh

Transcript of Keynote Presentation to the New Craft Future Voices
International Conference, 4–6 July, 2007, University of Dundee, Scotland.

It is nice to be here. I thought today that I would be somewhat contentious. I will raise a number of issues that I have articulated before in various places, but I hoped that the general thrust of what I have to say might help set a discursive tone to the proceedings.

It seems to me, having spent decades being wildly optimistic about the crafts, that in some respects it's about time we took a reality check. I was in Paris recently and on a nice bright sunny morning I strolled over to the Musée des Art Décoratifs, which had been recently reopened after six years of being restored, to have a look at some of my favourite decorative things. It was almost empty. After that, I went over to the Louvre to view some of my favourite paintings and I couldn't breathe for the crowds.

Let's be honest, the crafts or *les arts décoratifs*, or *applied arts*, or *ornamental arts*, or whatever we choose to call them at this time, have been more or less in a perpetual mixture of intellectual confusion, ideological chaos and institutional collapse, for at least three decades and probably more. All this is in stark contrast from the start of the twentieth century, when the Musée des Art Décoratifs was originally opened, amid fanfares and crowds. Perhaps the only real difference between the crafts, design and art at this time, in fact, is that the former is ailing, and the latter two are prospering.

As a category within the visual arts, the crafts have stayed alive largely for negative reasons. That is to say, nobody has managed to convincingly reallocate the practices contained within them to any other category within the arts. A significant number of practitioners we position within the crafts are actually ashamed to be so defined. In itself, that's a unique situation in the nomenclatic heritage of the arts. As I suggest, the good news is that, historically, it wasn't always like this. The later nineteenth century was a period in which the crafts confidently defined themselves, led the avant-garde in key respects, and enjoyed a rich, dense, historical and theoretical literature. There have been good moments since then and as always I very quickly add that there is interesting work and significant practice around the international scene. Nevertheless, I've come, myself, to find the tail-chasing circularity of the craft world to be deeply depressing. It seems to me that we need to radicalise our world before it's too late. Therefore I want to consider four things today, in an attempt to pull myself out of the nihilistic hole I have just dug.

First of all, given that I am a historian, I want to worry about the thorny problem of craft and modernity, which I think is the key to everything that accounts largely for the problems we are in. Secondly, I want to consider another industry that we all know and love – the history industry and how that affects the craft industries. Thirdly, I want to look at the crafts and postmodernity and then finally I am going to give a prognosis for the way forward, which will be the trickiest part.

Craft and Modernity

Many historians, I think, had been pondering over the last decade on what the term modernism means, and pondering even more on the meaning of postmodernism. There have been two major thrusts to this pondering: 1) to identify the successor to the clearly defunct postmodern period and 2) to articulate the relationship of craft to modernism. Both are of vital importance at this time. As an art historian who's been involved in the crafts for a long time, it struck me that we've an absolute need to describe and clarify the relationship of craft to modernism in a satisfactory way, before any of us within the craft world can move along in a meaningful way. From the perspective of people at this gathering, what is really striking is the very problematic nature, from the art historical viewpoint of the term, modern craft.

Modern, in its various linguistic derivatives, is perhaps the single most important cultural descriptor we have. In a number of publications over the last few years – in Garth Clark's work for example – it has been asserted 'that the arena in which all the visual arts have to reside is that of modernity'. He is right. Modernity is a fundamental among our colleagues within mainstream art history. Imagine the history of twentieth-century painting was not told from the perspective of modernity, or even from the point of view that modernity was only one thing amongst various other options. Leave out Picasso, Braque, Matisse, Miró, Mondrian, Pollock, Guston, Bacon *etc*, and see what kind of storyline you've got left. Alternatively, interlace all those artists into the storyline with all types of other artists, giving the same weight and credibility to all those academic portrait painters, historicists, folklorists, commercial mural artists, sign painters *etc*. What would the history of twentieth-century painting then read like? One might say, in some senses, it would be more interesting. Certainly it will be more sociologically accurate. But in most ways it will be a confused compromise mess of a history, without an intellectual or aesthetic core to it; it would not tell us why paintings look like they do in the twentieth century, or tell us anything about the grand poetic struggle of the best minds. Perhaps more important, it would fail to wire painting up to a larger world of ideas in other intellectual spheres. In other words, painting existed and thrived in the twentieth century, as part of the discourse of modernity, and very largely, the previous history of painting has been deliberately structured as a relational prelude to modern painting. I quickly add, I am not saying this is necessarily the right way to do it, I am simply saying that that is absolutely what has been done. In effect, without its function as a signifier of modernity, painting would lack a cohesive storyline.

That's where money and the power come into the picture. Every gallery, museum, dealership, private collector, auction house, publishing house and media organisation, insofar as they look at painting, have confirmed the economic and cultural power of that genre through its storyline, that is to say, the written and approved history of painting. Denied this pedigree, of a structured, logical history of aesthetic advance, it would become far more difficult to present and sell paintings.

And there is the rub – most definitions and historical musings on modernity over the last decades either leave out the concept of craft altogether, or if they include it, it's in the form of something outside of, and even a negation of the key concept: modernity. Craft is something that the *idea of the modern* leaves behind, or craft is something that was set up to resist the modern. This vision of craft is about the most damning thing that could happen to any practice in the visual arts – to be ignored in the project of modernity is to be denied space within the cultural hierarchy, and it largely explains the philosophical cultural and worst economic state of things in the crafts. This latter point can be a difficult thing to grasp, especially when put bluntly. So let's put it bluntly: the condition of written history and literature of craft is the single most powerful determinant in the ability of practitioners in the crafts to make a living. All that literary musing, ultimately, impacts on the economy.

How did this sorry state of affairs come to be? How did it happen? How did all these books on modern art, all those museums and galleries dedicated to modernism (beginning perhaps with the greatest of them all, the Museum of Modern Art, New York, founded in 1929), all those institutions that were set up to promote and make modernism popular, all those newspaper and magazine critics, professors of art history, television documentary directors, and collectors of modern art happen to forget modern craft? Put like that, it does seem really quite weird, not least because they managed to tell the 'modernist' story *of-just-about-everything-else* – painting, sculpture, architecture, city-planning, design – hundreds, and hundreds, and hundreds of times over. Is it because they didn't and don't think there was such a thing as modernist craft in the twentieth century? And if there wasn't actually a modernist craft defined in terms of the other modernist arts, then what of postmodernism? Strictly speaking, of course, we can wave goodbye to postmodern craft: you can't have a 'post' of a phenomenon that did not exist in the first place.

Let's assume modernity did not leave the crafts behind, and that the issue is one of identification and clarification, rather than invention. Of course, there is no one modernism as such in the visual arts but modernisms. The grand utopian modernisms that gave us abstraction and modern architecture and design, for example, were opposed and challenged by oppositional modernisms like surrealism and the ongoing expressionist tradition. I put it to you that there is another oppositional modernism among these, premised not on the newly uncovered psyche, or troubled sexuality, but on the politics of production and function of communal artistic expression. The modern craft movement was, in most respects, conceived of as a considered response to the conditions of modern life, and as such, it was a discourse aimed at complicating and changing the unfolding of the modernist projects. In this sense, a fully articulated theory of modern craft is not simply something to be bolted onto other existing modernisms: it is a modernism in its own right. We need also to clarify the relationship of the decorative arts to craft because in this sense, decorative art is not the same as craft, and the two are not synonymous. We also might conjecture that in those arts that have more developed sociological and anthropological dimensions than the fine arts, indeed that are premised on these discourses, modernity does not begin in the twentieth or even in the later nineteenth century, but is an ongoing project that began in the Enlightenment. Modernity in the crafts is intimately tied to the unfolding development of urban life, technology and mass consumption. It seems to me that the Enlightenment is a good moment from which the crafts can begin to articulate an appropriate modernism – a different modernism perhaps from the ones we are accustomed to.

The first thing to remind ourselves of as we face these crucial issues is that this is not, as such, a problem with its core in practice among the crafts people; practitioners did not create this problem of the absence of modern craft, it is a problem of historiography, and with the discipline of history generally, and of art history specifically.

The History Industry

The history industry, if you would like to call it that, is an enormous octopus-like creature in the middle of Western culture, which more or less dictates the cultural status of things. It's important to remember that there are considerably more historians at work in the Western world than there are professionals in the craft disciplines, and these historians collectively impinge on a very wide swathe of our cultural existence. The most obvious effect of history or practice is in simple mechanical terms. History provides the CV of a discipline, it records and orders its past and it allocates its significance to the various parts in it. In life, of course, without a good CV you don't get a job, and without a job, you are economically crippled. In the same way, the seriousness with which a discipline is regarded flows heavily from how it's been dealt with historically. For example, we accord infinitely greater significance to classical art than we do to folk art. The classical canon has dominated Western culture, and in key respects it continues to do so. We create our cities round classical plans and forms, we fill our museums with classical artefacts, and for hundreds of years, Western art has been premised on variations of classical themes. In short, the history industry has constructed and positioned classicism over a long period of time. This has had two effects: first, we allocate massively more significance to classicism than we do to folk art; everything which is broadly and loosely associated with classicism gains in economic, social and political value – classical art costs more than folk art because it embodies a larger historical project. In fact, we have arrived at the point at which we don't even consider classical artefacts in the same light as so-called folk artefacts: we keep them separate in our museums and universities, and in our minds, we have come to categorise them as being fundamentally of a different type.

The second way that history affects practice, and connected somewhat to the last point, is what might be termed the psychological. In the absence of a fully articulated dense and available history, practice in itself becomes more problematic. Making any kind of cultural artefact in a historical void, in an environment denied the nuances and symbols of a wider continuum, is inevitably more difficult. The analogy might be, I suppose, that history functions in relation to practice much in the way that memory mediates the behaviour of individual human beings. We act constantly in the knowledge of what we already know. What we know informs what we can or will know. What we know allows us to advance through life. Similarly, what a practice can collectively produce is mediated by what it has produced before, and the knowledge of what it has produced before. From that point of view, the crafts are suffering still from a kind of cultural Alzheimer's disease – practice doesn't have the fully integrated cultural memory to lean on as other disciplines do, and that provides us with enormous problems.

It could easily be argued that the later nineteenth and early twentieth centuries enjoyed a Golden Age in the crafts. What is also interesting is that the period also enjoyed a considerable and often brilliant literature that dealt with the crafts and material culture. Art Nouveau, the Secession, and the Arts and Crafts Movement, for example, were intellectually underpinned by some of the best cultural thinkers in Europe and North America. It is not coincidental that those worlds functioned in tandem.

This leads me back to modernism. History, of course, is not the same as the past. The past is what happened, whereas history is what we say about the past; the two are often very different. From this point of view, of course, it is up to the crafts to explore its past and construct the history that it wants and needs. One of the interesting observations from this perspective, taking me back to the idea that perhaps the history of craft – modern craft – should be told from the Enlightenment onwards, is that history as a discourse was largely invented during the Enlightenment, and is quintessentially itself a modern project. The material manifestation of history – the museum – was effectively an invention of the modern world, and exists essentially for two reasons – first, to save things that would otherwise have disappeared *ie* to preserve the material culture that modernisation would otherwise completely destroy, and second, the museum assists in the process of mapping the way forward – museums tell us where we've been, and then provide a platform for structured advance.

Postmodernity

Having worried a little bit about history and modernity, I want to move on to ponder on the issue of postmodernity. It seems to me that there are three core problems here I think, which I am sure you are all familiar with. I would label these: definitions, methodologies and ideology.

We've all spent 25 years playing that crushing, metaphysical party game worrying about the definition of craft: Am I a craftsperson, am I an artist, am I a designer? That mawkish pursuit, rooted not in structured, historically rooted argument but in anecdote and fallacy, need trouble us no more. Suffice it to reaffirm here, there is indeed no stable signifier 'craft', and there never has been. Needless to say, this unstable definition is a principal cause of what has for decades been an unstable and insecure craft world. Craft is a city built on a cultural fault line.

Methodology provides an interesting set of problems, as it is clear that we can't necessarily construct a craft history by appropriating the methods and structures of existing art history; the parameters are different. On contemplation of, say, a piece of ceramic, jewellery, or glass, one realises that in themselves they enjoy different historical motor-forces and parameters, and that these in turn are different from, say, the history of painting. For example, much pottery is characterised by being cheap, disposable, massively ubiquitous, and, partly because of these qualities, and because of the nature of the material, immensely durable. This makes pottery different not only from painting, but also different from jewellery.

The third issue, ideology, I will explain through a comparison: the work of Bernard Leach in relation to Ettore Sottsass, the Italian designer who created the company Memphis. Leach and Sottsass were contemporaries, and were both active in the ceramic field during the 1960s and 1970s. At that point in time, Bernard Leach was considered to be the seminal figure in the evolution of the modern studio craft movement. Ettore Sottsass, on the other hand, was a rather dangerous, brilliant Italian designer: the word craft never passed his lips. For most of us, the two figures, of the solid, spiritual, moralistic Englishman, and the sexy, irreverent, effervescent Italian, were utterly incompatible, and their differences were summed up materially in their work.

The problem is, that in the basic way their work was made, and in a number of the ideas they operated with, they had a surprisingly large amount in common. For example, in that period, both often did not make their own work. They made use of other potters, Sottsass obviously so, but when the pressure was on, Leach also didn't throw a considerable bulk of his own work, but other people made it for him. Secondly, Sottsass made use of local potters to hand-make his pots; he was interested in Italian Renaissance traditions, and in the way that tradition fused with wider issues. He was also on the left politically and very committed to the idea of a wider agenda for ceramics and his ceramic. Leach, as is widely known, was obsessed with hand-making, with local potters, historical traditions, and with left-wing ideas in relation to practice. In other words, the two shared quite a wide platform of ideas and practices. So what exactly is the difference between the two that has led us to place them in such very different worlds? The difference, I put it to you, is essentially ideological. There is nothing substantial to separate the two beyond ideology. The reason we tend to think that these two have less in common than Mother Teresa and Mike Tyson, is because of the ideologies surrounding design discourse, in relation to craft discourse. When you look at them closely, the material differences are actually far more ambivalent.

In Washington at the Corcoran Gallery, my colleagues and I staged several small internal colloquia to discuss the issue of postmodernism, in advance of beginning a process of organising an exhibition on that theme. After much debate, we (very crudely) managed to agree broadly that in our world, postmodernism happened roughly from the 1970s (no firm consensus); and we decided that postmodernism was substantially a negation or a rejection of certain forms of modernism, that is, of utopian idealist modernisms of the twentieth century. Interestingly, we also noted, as a group from a number of ethnic backgrounds, and as specialists in different areas of the visual arts, that the postmodern project, as it were, varied from culture to culture, and among different ethnic groups. For example, and to use a pertinent example, it seems to me that the way the post unfolded in Scotland is different in interesting ways from how it has unfolded in England.

If one looks at ethnic groups internationally, one realises that the post is a very complex creature, and has implications for class and gender as well as ethnicity. In all kinds of ways, an American postmodern exhibition must necessarily be different from a British one.

More interesting still, the post unfolds differently from discipline to discipline, powerfully so within the crafts. If one thinks of the key decade for postmodernism, the 1980s, what the jewellers were doing, for example, was very different from what the potters were doing. The jewellers tended to be far more political; they questioned the nature of materials; they explored body scarification and tattooing; they were interested in economics, ethnicity, sexuality, and class. The AIDS epidemic fuelled practice powerfully. By contrast, there were political ceramics, but actually, ceramics became more to do with the reappropriation of its own traditions, with the questioning, on the one hand, of the idea that ceramics was a sub-category of mainstream sculpture, and on the other, that a certain approach to the vessel was all that pottery could aspire to.

More generally, it seems to me that the post was about a return to ornamentation and decoration, and the reengagement with decoration as a *public* as opposed to a *private* discourse: necessarily because of this, it was based in eclecticism. Incidentally, I do believe that the idea of categorising arts through the idea of public and private practice is probably more use to us at this point in time than our existing modes of classification. But perhaps that is a paper for another time.

The New Humanism

Having been somewhat aggressive, I'd like to conclude by referring to the idea of the new humanism, which was in my title. I think there are a few things that we need to recognise. We must recognise that the term craft, as we usually deal with it, is quintessentially an Anglo-Saxon construct. It has no real basis beyond northern European and American cultures. It doesn't even make much sense in France: the term *métier* does not correspond meaningfully with the English *craft*; neither does the phrase *les arts décoratifs*. If we accept that, then the idea that there can be anything useful in imposing this existing nomenclature on India, China, Africa or Russia is frankly ridiculous. If craft is going to have a future as a defining term, and as a field worth thinking about, then it has to be repositioned in the new international environment.

Second, while government is pressuring us all – in a number of countries now – to show that our degree programmes and training schemes are generating wealth and jobs, we really must stop being silly about simply accruing and appropriating to our cause every single last practitioner, medium or company that might vaguely be defined as being to do with craft, in order to show that we are in a thriving cohesive sector. It might be good for propaganda, for getting government grants and for selling tartan, jam and love-spoons, but ultimately it doesn't help. It positions prosperity not as a reality but as a political myth, and it does nothing for the dynamism of the field.

Perhaps we should think about the next period in a different way. First and foremost, let's recognise that craft is several distinct constituencies once and for all. I suggest we recognise and bring into focus two constituencies: *poetry*, and *politics*.

Many within the craft disciplines engage in poetic discourse: they are about the making of physical things that engage the intellect and the emotions. We should simply recognise this and desist from further categorisation. If it works as poetry, it works. Why should it engage in anything beyond this? Let's embrace the idea of a poetic pot, chair, rug, or necklace and get on with it. This stuff is art, and it adds to the quality of life, to the aesthetic dimension, in its own way. Why complicate it more than this? Why bother placing wider socio-political burdens on it? As with most of you, I am passionate lover of certain periods and genres. I particularly care about ceramics; about metaphysical and early modern poetry; about Ancient (Classical) art; seventeenth-century Dutch art; fin de siècle fine and decorative art. These things sustain me, and I don't want to complicate my love of them with wider ideological and political agendas. Why should I?

Having said this, and secondly, I put it to you, that craft is indeed a political discourse, and has been throughout the modern period. Craft in this sense is engaged with modes of production, and attempts to have an impact on the socio-economic state of things, via culture. Of course, the great generation of practitioners, led by luminaries like William Morris and Henri Van de Velde, established a great tradition of politicised material culture, but the politics of making in the twenty-first century are different, and will demand different solutions from those of the nineteenth century. Perhaps more radically, craft production in this new sense might not imply the physical fabrication of anything. It might be more about infrastructure, economics and trade. The greatest challenges facing us – permanent unemployment, global poverty, religious and ethnic intolerance, illiteracy, mass ill-health, urbanism and the environment – are all haunting problems that a new ideology of craft could address. At the end of the nineteenth century, the agenda was set for craft to be concerned centrally with the augmentation of culture in the widest sense, in order that we might fundamentally improve the material fabric of existence. The world has been moving quickly since then. That idea of craft was configured in an age of steam and engineering. When that gave way to the age of oil (and caused the British Empire to give way to the American), the craft world – arguably – failed to respond by adjusting its intellectual and material parameters. Craft as a political ideal did not especially enjoy the twentieth century. We are now well into the electronic and communication age. What we need now is a politics of craft that can genuinely engage with the fragmented vortex that is the new globalism. Let's recognise the issues, and make a craft that is a vital creature capable of engaging with the world in a meaningful way. The great pioneers of the fin de siècle had a positivist strategy committed to the use of culture to transform society; they wanted to create a higher sense of civilisation. Not a bad agenda for a new humanism in the twenty-first century.

Developing a Participatory Craft Practice Approach

Frances Stevenson

This chapter offers insight into the development of a new method for practice-based research within textile design. The thesis will be completed in 2011.

It is generally acknowledged that contemporary makers work within a three-phase process: (1) initial stimulus, (2) development of the source and (3) realisation of the final product (Kettley, 2005). It is a systematic approach to craftwork, and can be explained in part through the increasing numbers of practitioners who undergo academic training (McAuley and Fillis, 2004) within academies that adhere to early Bauhaus pedagogic methods. Early Bauhaus had three stages within its curriculum: the preliminary instruction, the practical instruction and the architectural instruction (Wick, 2000). Walter Gropius' ideal and delivery of a preliminary course which placed an emphasis on individual creative exploration with the aim of finding oneself (and finding meaning), still exists in art schools today, and is part of a craft practitioner's practice. Practitioners store much of their creative influences, life experiences, experience of materials on which they continually build and reflect on alongside their ideals and their passions about life, within themselves (Paxon, 2007). This constitutes part of their personal knowledge. It is usually defined as tacit knowledge (Dormer, 1994). Through research conducted by others it is evident that the internal process is part of all crafts practice (Kettley, 2005; Stevenson and Scobie, 2007; Paxon, 2007). The ability to observe, depict and recognise form and content from a source is Bauhaus procedure (Wick, 2000) and the first phase of a contemporary craft maker's practice. There are also clear connections between stages two and three of the Bauhaus curriculum, current art school education and the craft-making process *ie* development of the source through materials, meaning workshop activity, and the translation of the materials into a final product.

A contemporary craft-making model that is based on a three-phase approach is presented here as the standard approach used by the majority of contemporary crafts practitioners who make work to sell.

Three phases that are generally regarded as the normal sequence of working within the craft-making approach are:

Phase **1** = Initial Stimulus and exploration of the stimulus

Phase **2** = Development through materials and prototype

Phase **3** = Realisation of final product

Each of the above phases is populated with 'activities', 'methods' and 'participants'. In Figure 1 and subsequent figures, Table 1 and the coding opposite.

A is the activity	Contemporary Craft Practice (CCP)	Participatory Craft Practice (PCP)
A1 The stimulus that provokes the initial sensation	The stimuli can be anything, a place or an object, for example. The stimulus can provoke an immediate response *ie* to record through drawing or photography. Or the stimuli may be 'stored' in the maker's memory for future use.	The stimuli are the prototype textiles.
A2 Exploration of ideas	This is often a sketchbook stage where ideas and possibilities become visible.	In PCP this is a playful approach to the prototypes, looking at possible outcomes.
A3 Product Development–Prototype	This refers to initial trials by the maker that result in prototypes or samples that inform the direction for the final product.	As in CCP, this refers to initial trials by the maker that result in prototypes or samples that inform the direction for the final product.
A4 Final Product	The final piece of work that is placed in the public domain.	As CCP. However, throughout this research prototypes were produced in order to hone the PCP process.
A5 Exhibition	The exhibition is the route through which the maker puts a final or realised product within the public domain.	The exhibition is the mechanism used to invite the public to interact with the prototypes.
A6 Reflection	Reflection is a key factor throughout all activities from 1–6. The purpose of identifying it at a key point in the stages is to highlight the break in a maker's cycle, *ie* between the cusp of finishing and prior to embarking on a new body of work. This involves an analysis of the work previously completed.	As is CCP, reflection is a key factor throughout all activities from 1–6.

Table 1.

A is the activity. This refers to the making process or the stages
that the participants go through, leading to a product outcome.

A1 The stimuli that provokes the initial sensation. In 'Contemporary Craft
Practice (CCP)' the stimuli can be anything, a place or an object, for example.
The stimuli can provoke an immediate response *ie* to record through drawing
or photography. Or the stimuli may be 'stored' in the maker's memory for
future use.

A2 Exploration of ideas
In CCP this is often a sketchbook stage where ideas and possibilities
become visible.

A3 Product Development–Prototype
In CCP this refers to initial trials by the maker that result in prototypes
or samples that inform the direction for the final product.

A4 Final Product

A5 Exhibition
In CCP the exhibition is the route through which the maker puts
a final or realised product within the public domain.

A6 Reflection
Reflection is a key factor throughout all activities from 1–6. The purpose of
identifying it at a key point in the stages is to highlight the break in a maker's
cycle, *ie* between the cusp of finishing and prior to embarking on a new body
of work. This involves an analysis of the work previously completed.

The diagrams should be read like a clock face, *ie* the starting point for each
event starts at 12 o'clock and moves clockwise. For the purposes of this
research, activities are contained within each of the three phases of the CCP
model. Each phase also identifies who is involved in the activity (the participant) and what approach is taken in carrying out the activity (the method).

In Figure 1, and subsequent figures, **M** is the methods.
This is the approach taken, to carry out the activity.

M1 Independent – only one person was involved in the activity.

M2 Collaboration – two or more people were working together with
a fixed aim.

M3 Interaction – two or more people were involved in an open session of play
and development with no boundaries or fixed outcome.

P are the participants – people who are involved in the activity.

P1a and **P1b** Practitioners.

P2 Public.

This is the initial idea, or recognisable sense, that 'something' may be worth exploring. This may evolve through reflection on previous work, or it may be a new experience that has been seen, touched, read or heard by the maker. Whatever the source, it provokes a response in the form of an action. The maker's action captures the essence of the 'provocateur' in various ways, *ie* drawing, filming, photographing or recording (see activity 1 in *Figure 1*). All of these serve to internalise the stimulus for the maker. This then becomes the creative stimulus throughout the entire process (Kettley, 2005).

A key factor at this point is the maker's engagement with the stimulus (Yanagi, 1972), as the whole experience of sensing and recording becomes the maker's creative spark that is waiting to be ignited. The following excerpt helps to explain this using storytelling as its method:

> *Think of something in your life that you do, or that you participate in, or a place that you go that can fill you with an anticipatory joy just at the thought of it, and you will understand my passion for drawing. Drawing is central to my creative practice and I believe that it expresses the whole emotional and visual experience of the person at a moment in time. When I am 'there' in a rural setting drawing, there is an interaction between the environment, the materials and me that is fluid and unstoppable (both physical and psychological), between the movements of the hand and the eye, and the decision making of the brain. Nature is the driver to my creativity and the wilder it is the hungrier I am to capture it. I have no fear about placing marks and colours on the paper's surface and risky decisions about what? where? how? merely add to the thrill. The feeling of space and beauty enthrals me and I feel small in nature's vastness but at the same time exhilarated that I am a part of it, allowing myself the indulgence, at least for those moments, to immerse myself in the colours, textures, shapes, sounds and smells that surround me. (Stevenson and Scobie, 2007: 129)*

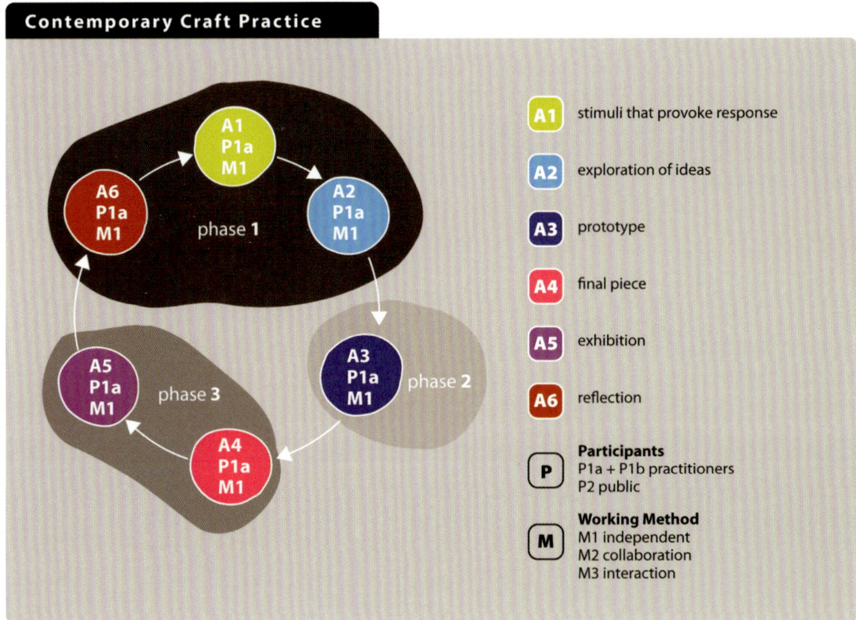

Figure 1. Contemporary Craft Practice.

This helps us understand the sensory engagement with the stimulus at the very outset of the maker's process. The maker is identifying 'anticipatory joy' at the thought of venturing into nature's landscape, and looks forward to an experience that is about to happen. The next quote moves on into the exploration stage where the maker begins to play with the information collected (see activity 2 in *Figure 1*).

> *I return to my drawings that contain the marks, colours and emotions of the drawing trip. I pin the work around me to remind me of the experience and I search for shapes, marks and colours in the drawings to pull out and reform into arrangements that intimate a visual harmony when viewed but still contain the life of the source. Spontaneity is still the key here, although I recognise that at the drawing stage I see the arrangements of potential textile designs in my head...*
> (Stevenson and Scobie, 2007: 131)

In Figure 1, stimuli that provoke response (A1), exploration of ideas (A2) and reflection (A6) are identified as activities that form the first phase of the craft process.

Phase 2 Development through materials and prototype

The development stage involves development of primary information from Phase 1 in order to explore creative possibilities. It is a playful stage and it is also a risk taking stage that moves between sketched ideas and material development through workshop activity. The maker allows their creative judgement, knowledge and experience to guide them at this stage (Dormer, 1994, citing Janik, 1988; Pye, 1995). In the current research, Phase 2 engenders cloth samples that can be draped and handled in order to judge the aesthetic integrity.

Phase 3 Realisation of final product

The third stage is the production of final craft products that can be placed within the public domain to be publicly assessed (Dormer, 1994). This assessment can simply be the purchase of the work by the public or endorsement through galleries. This phase represents the coming together of all the previous stages and incorporates activities A4 and A5 in the Contemporary Craft Practice Model.

Key points from the contemporary craft practitioner approach

Being a maker of contemporary craft is a solitary occupation. Throughout all of the activities within the contemporary craft model there is only one participant in the entire making process (the maker) until the exhibition stage in Phase 3. Evidence shows that predominantly practitioners work alone: 84 per cent of professional makers of contemporary craft are defined as 'sole traders' (McAuley and Fillis, 2002, 2004). However, evidence also shows that 68 per cent of practitioners would like the opportunity to work with someone else (McAuley and Fillis, 2004).

Stages one and two are the most important stages in the process in terms of innovation and new product development. However the storytelling excerpt provides some evidence of how the practitioner tends to visualise their products at an early stage, ' ... I see the arrangements of potential textile designs in my head ... ' suggesting that there is scope to challenge makers' thinking and their own preconceptions regarding what they should be producing. Challenging thinking at an earlier stage is key here, since there is no feedback for makers until the final product is made and put out for public 'judgement'.

The Participatory Craft Practice (PCP) approach questions the approach of working in isolation, and proposes instead a means of both engaging the public and challenging makers' thinking in order to develop a more dynamic method of working for mid-career makers of craft.

Participatory Craft Practice: Process, Methods and Data Collection

There are four studies that have been central to the PCP approach in its development stages, and each study has used the researcher's own printed textiles practice (see *Figure 2*). This is appropriate since the researcher fits the contemporary craft maker profile (Crafts Council, 2010) and was at a stage in her career where a 'creative injection' was needed. The researcher is a participant immersed in the process of making, method development and analysis (Robson, 1993).

Figure 2. Hand-painted silk velvet scarves by Frances Stevenson (2000).

Each of the studies in the development of PCP has been recorded and analysed using various methods. They include taped conversations, film and photography. In this essay the visual record of the process is being used through diagrams and photography to explain how the participatory approach has evolved to this point.

Essentially PCP has evolved through a series of studies that explore what practical and beneficial methods might better inspire innovation and new product development, through challenging the maker's thinking. PCP also investigates alternative approaches to practice that involve participants other than the maker. The aim of each study was to work with people in order to develop a process that would be suitable for contemporary craft practitioners' work. The studies enabled participants to inspire each other through how they played with the prototypes/probes (Gaver, et al, 2004) and through how they each responded. The current researcher placed a great deal of emphasis on the sensory aspect of the participant's knowledge, as the sense of touch and sight are fundamental to the success of printed textile cloth products (Potvin, 2007).

The studies are in sequence and each builds one on the other.

PCP extends the contemporary craft-making range of activities, methods and participants, in the current studies as shown below and in Table 1.

A1 The stimulus that provokes the initial sensation
In 'Participatory Craft Practice' the stimuli are the prototype textiles.

A2 Exploration of ideas
In PCP this is a playful approach to the prototypes, looking at
possible outcomes.

A3 Product Development–Prototype
As in Contemporary Craft Practice, this refers to initial trials by the maker that result in prototypes or samples that inform the direction for the final product.

A4 Final Product

A5 Exhibition
In PCP the exhibition is the mechanism used to invite the public to interact with the prototypes

A6 Reflection
As is Contemporary Craft Practice, reflection is a key factor throughout all activities from 1–6.

PCP Study One: New Craft – Future Voices

This study involved two makers who came together to develop new work. Both makers had reached a creative block, meaning they were tired of producing the same 'type' of work and needed to reinvigorate their craft practice. In order to move their practice and thinking on, they collaborated with each other on a project and sought to engage the audience with their products at the exhibition stage.

The practitioners' aim was to understand how they each approached and moved through their own creative process in the disciplines of ceramics and printed textiles. By sharing their knowledge and experience through working together, they aimed to discover how, and if, an exchange of approaches could affect the outcomes while working as a team, and to what extent the collaboration could inform:

·   The experience of generating new ideas and concepts,
    particularly in relation to pattern and form.

·   New knowledge realised through exploring material and technologies, and
    exploration through the intellectual tension between 2D print and 3D ceramics.

·   The final outcome and the artwork produced.

The following methods were used by the practitioners to develop work:

Drawing – the researchers worked together in order to exchange the knowledge of their independent approaches. They discussed their emotional responses to their environment as well as their reasons for choosing their visual source and the materials used. *Dialogue* – throughout the research it became clear that interaction was vital in discovering similarities and differences in approaches and thoughts. However, the researchers discovered that technical 'how to' language was not wholly appropriate when discussing their experience and used storytelling and gestures in order to explain their thoughts. *Literature* – some relevant texts were discussed throughout the research so that the researchers could share theoretical knowledge underpinning nature and craft. *Photography* – all of the sessions were documented photographically along with work produced. *Video recording* – the development of ideas was recorded in order to observe the collaborative process.

The participants in this study included the researcher, a ceramicist and the public who become participants at the exhibition stage.

The craft produced from the collaboration was presented as a familiar domestic ritual, *ie* a table with cloth pieces and ceramics, and people were asked to set the table. The pieces in the exhibit were decorated with a range of colours and patterns and the objective of the research was to explore how the participants responded to the decorative elements through their arrangement of them on the table. The settings were photographed by the participants and used for analysis by the researcher (see *Figure 3*).

This initial study was the catalyst to a series of other studies as it presented a method of exploring (using the public in an exhibition environment) alternative directions for the researcher's work through the participants' actions. In producing the work itself the researchers worked creatively and did generate new ideas and concepts through taking more risks when using different methods and new materials *ie* paper, sunlight and a video camera. Therefore it exposed the makers to a new collaborative method of working. However, the textiles practitioner found that the sharing of tacit knowledge hindered her development at the time as 3D form development was new and ideas needed internalisation time to mature.

If we look at Figure 4 we can see that it is not dissimilar to Figure 1 in that the phases are in the same sequence. The participants and working methods have changed with more collaborators and public participation, and different working methods driving the innovation and inspiration agenda.

Figure 3. New Craft – Future Voices Exhibition pieces. Textiles by Frances Stevenson and Ceramics by Lara Scobie (2007).

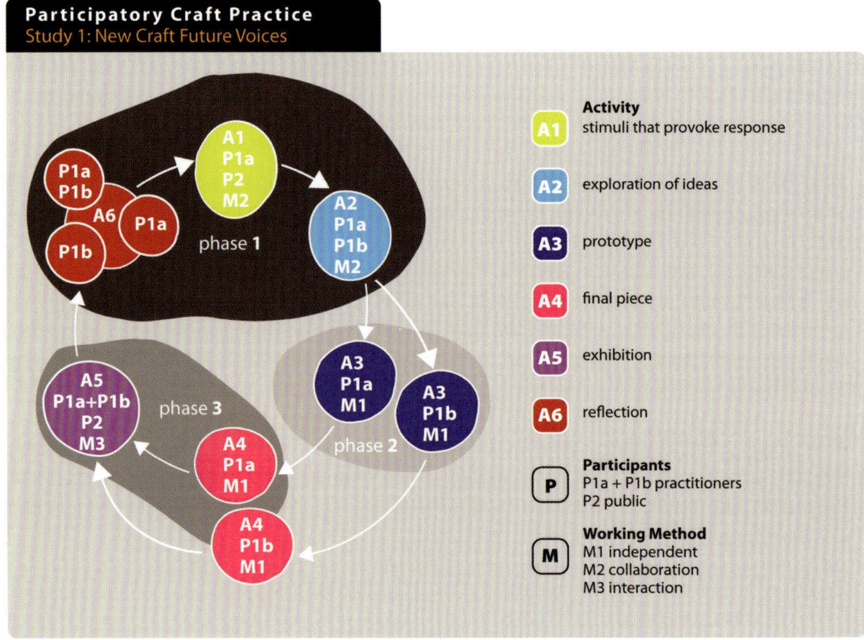

Figure 4. Practice Evolved in Study One: New Craft – Future Voices.

The aim of this project was to trial a method of inquiry about how the public 'felt' about the researcher's textile products, focusing on sensory responses. The sensory response stems from an anthropological perspective that refutes the perception that sensory experience and knowledge are simply physical responses emerging from an individual's personal experience. This research argues through the case studies, that sensory experience and sensory knowledge are areas of cultural expression that underpin the values and practices of society (Howes, 2003). This is significant as the contemporary craft maker generally seeks to develop products for a marketplace and not individual people.

This study again used the exhibition as the vehicle to present the pieces, which were a body of finished textiles from the past, and a body of prototype samples that had no clear function. The researcher interacted with the public this time by asking questions about their thoughts and aspirations for the work. The aim was to find out how they connected with the work and what they felt they could or would use the pieces for.

The questions were open and deliberately thought-provoking. They were intended to challenge the audience's thoughts about the sensory value (if any) of the textile products they were interacting with. There were four questions asked:

·   What primary sensation do you experience?

·   What strikes you as significant about these textiles?

·   What emotion(s) do these textiles stimulate in you?

·   What meaning(s) do you attach to these textiles?

The responses were recorded and the actions of the participants photographed.

Past work and new prototype pieces were placed in an exhibition space to ascertain at what stage in a product's development it is more beneficial for the practitioner to probe for an audience response, particularly in terms of how the practitioner can utilise the information to facilitate new product development.

The public preferred the prototype pieces as they offered opportunities for play. Although the questions challenged them, they became more engaged with the products as they thought deeply about their response. The participants often talked about memories and stories from their past that they connected with emotionally, and which influenced their decisions and feelings about a product. The questions seemed to help play develop. The aspect of play became the key as it sparked new ideas in terms of the new potential products for the maker.

For this study the craft phases changed, with Phase 2 being the starting point using textile prototypes as the research tools, as illustrated in Figure 5. There was also deep reflection and emotional responses from the public as they were questioned about the products, and this generated opportunities for future products with the maker.

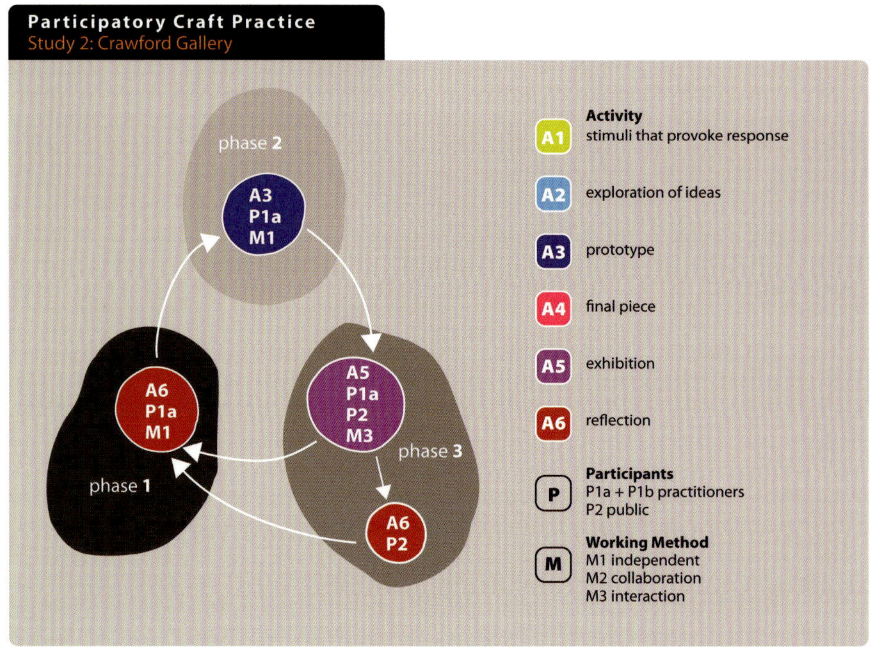

Figure 5. Practice Evolved in Study Two: Crawford Gallery Exhibition.

PCP Study Three: One to One

The aim of this study was to move the colours, patterns and cloth into a 3D context, *ie* the body. This was a small study that arose from one of the outcomes of study two: the participants, continuous placing of the cloth prototypes on their bodies.

Two people were invited to work with the researcher and the textile prototypes in order to place and arrange them on their bodies (see *Figure 6*).

This proved very effective in moving forward the practitioner's product development thinking. Through this study she started to visualise pattern compositions in 3D contexts. This was one of the objectives from the first study, but it was only the action of working with 'real bodies' that enabled her to begin thinking in this way (see *Figure 7*).

PCP Study Four: Making it Happen

The researcher used the exhibition framework (*Figure 8*) once again to explore audience interaction with the prototypes. This time she asked participants to interact but did not actively take part herself. The aim was to ascertain the effectiveness of audience participation without the maker questioning or without 'familiarity' as in the domestic table.

Although this proved effective as an exhibition piece, providing good critic feedback, it was less effective as a means of moving on the maker's thinking as the public needed the prompts, *ie* someone to interact and 'play' with, and the maker needed to be able to interact with them (see *Figure 9*).

Figure 6. Practitioner and participant 'playing' with the textile prototypes (2009). Photography by Malcolm Finnie.

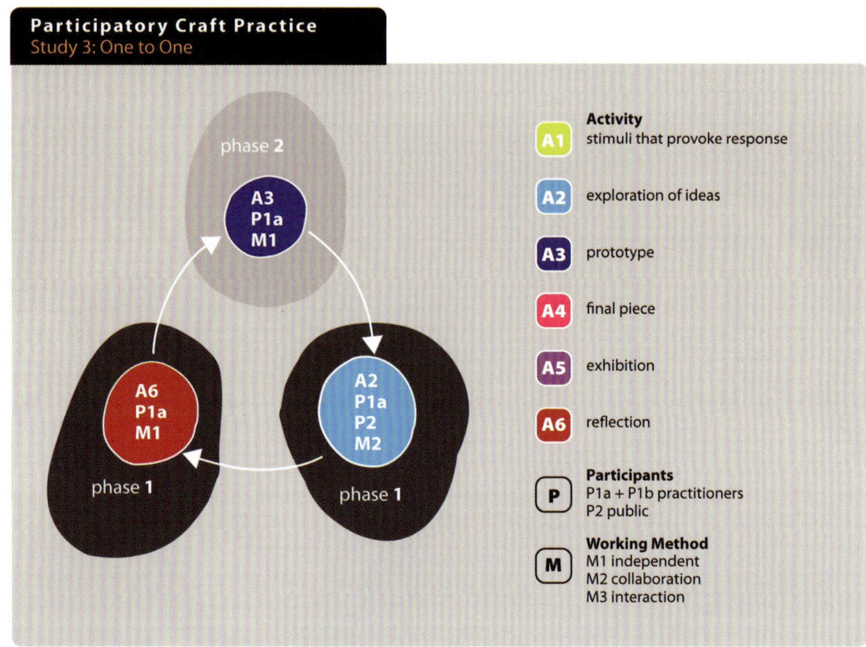

Figure 7. Practice Evolved in Study Three: One to One.

Discussion[2]

Participatory Craft Practice is a new paradigm for craft in that it presents alternative working methods and approaches for practitioners that engage the public, through the exhibition. The figures presented in the paper show how the PCP approach intervenes and contributes at the product development stages of a practitioner's process in order to generate new ideas and concepts for the maker.

The PCP rationale for an alternative or different approach for craft practice stems from the researcher's experience of working in the professional contemporary craft sector and the need for continuous product innovation that the sector requires. It is clear that innovation and the ability to diversify and develop new work are crucial, and this has been acknowledged as being at the core of the professional practitioner's business (Creative and Cultural Skills, 2009).

PCP provides craft practitioners with an alternative approach to innovation and new product development that can be adopted when needed. It is an intervention that takes place at stage two of craft practice, the product development stage. This is the crucial 'middle' stage where the practitioner reflects from past experiences whilst being actively involved in material development, and visualisation of new products. PCP allows the maker's thinking to diversify in a natural way through 'play' with participants. This allows for the unexpected through the way that participants interact with the maker's prototypes, bringing inspiration to the practitioner and engaging the public with craft. In the studies presented here as part of the development of PCP, the author examines the role of users as participants in the product development stage. In doing so, the users/participants of textiles become the critics and advisors of possibilities that inspire the maker. Participatory Craft Practice in this context is collectively conceived craft products. The professional craft maker's response is innovative product development for the marketplace.

Figure 8. Making it Happen Exhibition, which accompanied the V&A
at Dundee conference, Dalhousie Building, University of Dundee, 2009.

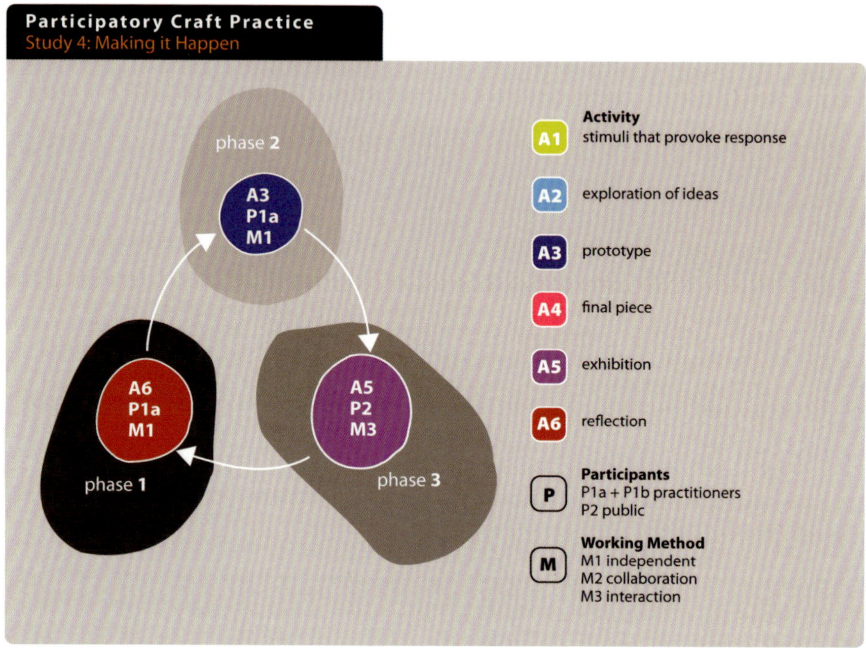

Figure 9. Practice Evolved in Study Four: Making it Happen.

The paper demonstrates how new working methods for contemporary craft practice, through methods of engagement with users of textiles participating in design practice, have been explored.

Participatory craft advocates that sensory knowledge is fundamental to the development and market success of textile products and the PCP approach explores the way in which the participants' sensory knowledge and experience as potential users of textiles can be a source of innovation for the professional crafts practitioner. The paper demonstrates that sensory knowledge can be assimilated by the maker within the PCP process.

Users are an important part within the PCP process

The essay identifies how crafted objects can be used as research tools to aid new product development in a professional crafts arena. It also identifies how engaging a sensory approach can facilitate appropriate methods of user participation in new product development. It identifies how the professional craft sector can be strengthened through collaboration and public engagement.

This research contributes to the continuing evaluations of Craft Practice and the contribution of craft to the creative economy and puts forward Participatory Craft, its ideal and its methods, as a potential model for sustaining innovation within a small business. It also has implications for selling, working, teaching and exhibiting craft through collaborative practice.

This essay began by discussing the need for craftspeople to have sustainable livelihoods, and PCP is proposed as a working collaborative method that can help sustain innovation.

Collaboration is a key here and we can find evidence of the benefits of exploring new collaborative working methods through practitioners themselves (McAuley and Fillis, 2004) and through working ventures such as the Australian 'Smartworks'.

New technologies, new manufacturing centres, and changing marketplace preferences are encouraging some craftspeople to revisit ideas to do with design, industry and the handmade. (Cochrane, 2007: 63)

The projects in 'Smartworks' put Dormer's model of distributed knowledge into practice. Smartworks demonstrates through gathered evidence that it is the practitioner's personal know how that empowers them to take charge of technology and technological processes. There seems to be a philosophy that has craftspeople, business and the public work together in order to achieve better prospects for the individual and for the cultural profile of their respective countries. Practitioners adopt alternative ways of working, giving them diversity and bringing craft into different design spheres. The PCP approach also aspires to a philosophy that has practitioners, business and the public working together.

Notes

[1] Crafts Council criteria are being used for this research. They state that to be eligible to register as a crafts practitioner with them, applicants must meet at least one of the following criteria '(1) ... *produce contemporary craft work that is cutting edge and ensures the highest standard of workmanship... (2) produce work that does not seek to reproduce or restore, but rather be innovative in its use of materials and aesthetic vision... (3) produce work that not only reflects your individual signature but also demonstrates investigation of processes and critical enquiry.'* (Crafts Council website)

[2] The PCP approach is in an evolutionary stage. Therefore a discussion seemed more appropriate than a conclusion in order to highlight the extent of the work so far.

Further Reading

Cochrane, G. (2007) Australia and New Zealand: Design and the Handmade. In: Alfoldy. S. (ed.) *NeoCraft: Modernity and the Crafts.* Halifax, The Press of the Nova Scotia College of Art and Design. pp. 63–81.

Crafts Council (2010). *The National Register of Makers.* [Online] Available from: http://www.craftscouncil.org.uk/explore-craft/national-register-of-makers [Accessed 17 March 2010].

Creative and Cultural Skills & The Crafts Council (2009) *The Craft Blueprint. A Workforce Development Plan for Craft in the UK.* London, UK.

Dormer, P. (1994) *The Art of the Maker: Skill and Its Meaning in Art, Craft and Design.* UK: Thames and Hudson.

Gaver, W. W., Boucher, A., Pennington, S., Walker, B. (2004) *Cultural Probes and the Value of Uncertainty.* [Online] Available from: http://www.gold.ac.uk/interaction/public/ [Accessed 17 March 2010].

Howes, D. (2003) *Sensual Relations: Engaging the Senses in Culture and Social Theory.* USA: The University of Michigan Press.

Janik, A., (1988) Tacit knowledge, working life and scientific method. In Goranzon, B. and Josefson, I. (eds.) *Knowledge skill and artificial intelligence.* Berlin and Heidelberg: Springer-Verlag. 62-3.

Kettley, S. (2005) Crafts Praxis as Design Resource. In the Proceedings of the Fifth Engineering and Product Design in Education Conference. Napier University, September 2005 Edinburgh UK. *Available from: http://www.sarahkettleydesign.co.uk/sarahkettley/publications_sarah_kettley_.html* EPDE 2005 Crossing Design Boundaries. *[Accessed 8 March 2010].*

McAuley, A. and Fillis, I. (2002) *Crafts Businesses in Scotland: a study.* Report for the Scottish Arts Council, Scottish Enterprise and Scottish Enterprise Glasgow, Glasgow.

McAuley, A. and Fillis, I. (2004) *Making it in the Twenty-first Century: a socio-economic study of craftspeople in England and Wales 2003/2004*. Report for Crafts Council and Arts Councils of England and Wales, London.

Paxon, A. (2007) Jerwood Applied Arts Prize: Jewellery exhibition recording. 12 October 2007–March 2008. National Museum of Scotland, Chambers Street, Edinburgh.

Potvin. J. (2007) Lost in translation: Georgio Armani and the textualities of touch. In: Alfoldy. S., [ed]. *NeoCraft: Modernity and the Crafts*. Halifax, Canada: The Press of the Nova Scotia College of Art and Design, 83–98.

Pye, D. (1995). *The Nature and Art of Workmanship*. Britain: Herbert Press.

Robson, C. (1993) *Real World Research: a resource for social scientists and practitioner-researchers*. Oxford: Blackwell Publishers.

Stevenson, F. and Scobie, L. (2007) Natural forces – dynamic ingredients for creative practice. In: Follett, G. and Valentine, L. [eds.] *New Craft – Future Voices. Proceedings of the International Conference. 4–6 July 2007*. Dundee, Scotland: Duncan of Jordanstone College of Art and Design. 123–133.

Wick, R.K. (2000) *Teaching at the Bauhaus*. Germany: Hatje Cantz Verlag.

Yanagi, S. (1972) *The Unknown Craftsman*. Japan: Kodansha International.

Zimmermann, E. (2003) Play as Research: The iterative design process. In: Laurel, B. (ed.) *Design Research Methods and Perspectives*. Massachusetts USA: Massachusetts Institute of Technology. pp. 176–184.

Profiling the Behaviour
of People Working with Craft
Ian Fillis

Introduction

Craft is taken to mean an object which must have a high degree of hand-made input, but not necessarily having been produced or designed using traditional materials, produced as a one-off or as part of a small batch, the design of which may or may not be culturally embedded in the country of production, and which is sold for profit. (Fillis, 2000)

Historically, the craft enterprise can be traced to medieval times (Heslop, 1997), the Italian Renaissance (Welch, 1997), the Arts and Crafts period (Naylor, 1971) through to the present day (Knott, 1994; Fillis, 2003; Fillis, 2008). The nature and meaning of craft has altered, from its early vernacular status to the more recent aesthetic appreciation of the craft product (Aslin, 1981). A difficulty in tracing the development of craft as a recognised industry is that there is a lack of consensus regarding its definition (Dormer, 1997). Metcalf (1997) makes the distinction between craft as skilful labour and craft as a class of objects involving a high degree of manual input, either by using the hand itself, hand tools and even hand-held power tools. The craft object does not necessarily have to be produced using traditional materials, only that conventional methods should have been used as part of the production process. Now, in the post-industrialisation era, the craftsperson has to compete with both domestic and overseas competition where many products appear hand-crafted even though they are often mass-produced using advanced technological processes. Contemporary literature suggests that crafts be viewed as part of the cultural and creative industries comprising fields such as book publishing, music, television and radio broadcasting, independent film and video, the art trade and cinema (Gray and McGuigan, 1993; Myerscough, 1996; Hesmondhalgh, 2002).

When examining craft businesses in Scotland, England and Wales, the definitions used by the relevant support organisations vary: the crafts section of the Small Business Division of the now defunct Scottish Development Agency viewed crafts in a wider sense than the Crafts Council of England and Wales, covering factory-based batch production as well as workshop production of one-off designs (Forbes and Munro, 1988). The Craftworks survey (Leeke, 1994) defined crafts broadly, from individuals to enterprises making a functional or decorative product which has a handmade element at some stage in its production. Coopers and Lybrand (1994) distinguished between the production of hand craft and craft-based industries involved in larger scale manufacturing practices. The craft product itself must exhibit aesthetic appeal, be of individual design and contain a large degree of manual skill in its production. It is the Metcalf (1997) definition which the author adopts, but with the additions that the craft is sold for profit and that it may or may not be culturally embedded in the country of production. The craft enterprise grows via the use of design and business competencies which have overriding knowledge-based foundations (Fillis, 2000). Healy (2002) evaluates the new economic era where knowledge and innovation are often more important than the ability to engage in mass production and where individual skills and creativity are viewed as drivers of globalisation. Creativity is not just applicable to the craft itself but also to the entrepreneurial thinking and resultant innovation in developing the craft enterprise (Collaborative Economics, 2001).

Internationalisation of Craft

Many craft enterprises focus their activities solely on the domestic market while others also engage internationally. Therefore it is useful to gain an understanding of the mechanisms behind internationalisation which is the outward movement of an individual enterprise or larger grouping (Johanson and Vahlne, 1977). The term international can refer to an attitude of managers of the enterprise relating to overseas activities or the actual process by which it carries out these activities. International experience also affects the attitudes of the key decision makers involved. Lack of knowledge and resource limitations tend to prevent the enterprise from growing. As experience and knowledge increase, culturally distant markets are more likely to be developed. Additional factors which impact on the process include the industry type, the product and the particular cultural characteristics of the domestic and overseas markets. What is also required is an understanding that process should be viewed as change, and that it should also be recognised that not all craft enterprises are, or indeed want to be, internationally oriented.

In addition to the artistic competencies which contribute to internationalisation, entrepreneurial marketing capabilities also play a part. One way of understanding how these factors are operationalised is to construct profiles of those working in the craft enterprise (Fillis, 2000; 2002a, b, c; 2004; 2007; 2008). Part of this profiling involves the incorporation of business and artistic forms of creativity which enable the small enterprise with limited resources to gain competitive advantage in the marketplace. The nature of international markets is changing, with globalisation and easier access to existing and new markets being major factors. Instant internationals can now enter and grow their activities much more quickly than previously modelled (Bell *et al*, 2004; Knight and Cavusgil, 2004; Rialp *et al*, 2005). Physical and perceptual barriers to internationalisation can be overcome through the use of the Internet (Hamill and Gregory, 1997; Matlay, 2004); for example, low cost access to market research and less dependence on agents and distributors. Improved communications can also increase profitability levels. Internationalisation through networking can be achieved by establishing and building relationships in new markets and also by connecting to existing networks in other countries (Johanson and Mattson, 1988; Keeble *et al*, 2004).

Using the Entrepreneurial Marketing Construct to Understand Craft Behaviour

The interrogation of the interface between marketing and entrepreneurship enhances understanding of craft enterprise behaviour by focusing on the informal and creative mechanisms of securing artistic and business growth (Carson *et al*, 1995; Collinson and Shaw, 2001; Fillis, 2002d). Many organisations carry out their activities using highly informal, unstructured, reactive mechanisms while others develop, over time, a proactive and skilled approach where innovation and identification of opportunities result in a competitive edge. At the two ends of the continuum, formal marketing involves highly structured, sequential decision making while entrepreneurial decisions tend to be haphazard and opportunistic. The marketing/entrepreneurship interface deals with areas of commonality such as analytical skills, judgement, positive thinking, innovation and creativity. The issue of creativity is especially relevant here, given the nature of the craft sector, where innovative product design and originality in business approach can give the enterprise a competitive advantage in both domestic and overseas markets.

Research Methodology

In order to help develop a profile of those working in the craft sector, a pluralistic methodology was adopted, incorporating both qualitative and quantitative approaches where research bias was minimised by methodological triangulation (Gill and Johnson, 1991). Complementary data were acquired from a postal survey and in-depth interviews. This enabled internal cross-checking to be carried out and increased the credibility of the data. The study itself involved assessing the beliefs, attitudes and behaviour of small craft enterprise owner/managers in the United Kingdom and the Republic of Ireland. The initial postal survey used mostly structured and semi-structured questions, with a limited number of open-ended questions and various measurement scales (Kidder and Judd, 1986; Oppenheim, 1992). This was pre-tested to ensure the structure, language and overall design were appropriate to the needs of the research. The in-depth interviews were based around a number of themes and recorded. Once the data were collected, analysis took the form of both a statistical approach using descriptive and inferential techniques (Bryman and Cramer, 1997) and a more qualitative content analysis (Kolbe and Burnett, 1991).

Organisation-level factors investigated included the numbers employed, length of time in exporting, exporting as an expansion strategy, the value of annual export sales, total annual sales and the current state of exporting, attitudes, motivation and impediments towards exporting. The second stage involved follow-up interviews with 30 exporting and non-exporting craft owner/managers in order to validate the initial findings and also to explore additional themes relating to initial business start-up and exporting activities: the problems encountered when selling in both domestic and overseas markets; the level of business and marketing competencies; the relevance of establishing networks and developing relationships; the main markets served; the methods adopted in selling the craft product and an appraisal of the current state of business in general. The interviews were drawn to a close with the respondent discussing the future direction of the business.

Sampling Approach

One of the main reasons for carrying out the quantitative study before any extensive qualitative data collection was that when data collection was taking place, an all-encompassing directory or database of craft enterprises did not exist from which to sample respondents. A further reason for carrying out the quantitative work initially was the desire to identify exporting and non-exporting craft enterprises from which a further sample would be taken for qualitative in-depth interviewing. A range of publications, organisations and individuals were consulted before sampling was carried out. The most useful compilations were those by organisations such as the Crafts Councils. These sources identified 3037 high-quality craft enterprises. A representative random sample of 500 craft businesses was selected from the lists, with cross-checking carried out to ensure sample units were not repeated. The number of usable responses was 27 per cent, comparable to studies in other sectors (Bilkey, 1982; Hart *et al*, 1994). Initial descriptive statistical analysis was carried out on the postal questionnaire data, followed by various inferential procedures (Anderson *et al*, 1996). This was then followed by a qualitative analysis of the in-depth interviews where the findings were compared and contrasted with the initial quantitative study. Triangulation of the quantitative and qualitative data facilitated the construction of the profiles.

Approaching one half of all respondents (47.5 per cent) operate on an individual basis. Over one third employ between two and five people, indicating that the vast majority operate in a microenterprise environment. This compares with statistics from the Department of Trade and Industry (2002) which identified 68.3 per cent of all businesses as sole operations. The latest available figures show that microenterprises comprise 95.7 per cent of all businesses (Department for Business Innovation and Skills, 2009). Benchmarking the crafts with other industries, the divisions of 'other mining and quarrying', 'manufacture of food products and beverages', and 'manufacture of leather and leather products' consist of lower percentages of self-employed owner/manager businesses. Industry divisions with higher percentages include 'manufacture of tobacco products, and 'manufacture of chemicals and chemical products'. Although there are no Department of Trade and Industry statistics which directly relate to the craft sector, it is possible to deduce that divisions such as 'publishing, printing and reproduction of recorded media', 'manufacture of wearing apparel' and 'manufacture of textiles' are related fields to the craft and creative industries. According to the most recent UK Government statistics, small and medium-sized enterprises (SMEs) in general account for 99.9 per cent of all enterprises, with over one million businesses falling under the microenterprise category (Department for Business Innovation and Skills, 2009). Small businesses in general have been the main source of new jobs in the UK and elsewhere for many years (Fielden *et al*, 2000). Reaching a detailed understanding of the craft enterprise has direct implications for organisations of a similar size across sectors.

Well over half of respondents (58.8 per cent) recorded total annual sales of less than £30,000. More than 10 per cent experienced sales of between £30,001 and £50,000, while over 13 per cent had sales of between £50,001 and £100,000. At the other end of the scale, 6.7 per cent of respondents had secured sales of over £500,000. Respondents were asked to indicate the level of annual sales generated through exporting. Well over half of exporters achieved export sales of less than £10,000, with over one fifth achieving sales of between £10,001 and £25,000. At the other end of the range, five exporters achieved sales of over £100,001, with three reaching in excess of £250,000. Exports, on average, accounted for just over 38 per cent of total sales. These figures compare favourably with previous surveys by Bruce and Filmer (1983), Knott (1994), Leeke (1994), Coopers and Lybrand (1994) and Myerscough (1996). Respondents were asked to identify the markets to which they were currently exporting. General geographical areas were selected, rather than specific countries. The most popular export destinations were the European Union and North America, although there were several emerging markets including Japan, Korea and Singapore. Analysis of export destination by country of origin of the exporter showed differences in the markets chosen. Exporters from Northern Ireland and the Republic of Ireland tended to concentrate on exporting within Europe and North America. Export market choice is in part determined by the 'Celtic factor', where culturally-close export markets are chosen (O'Grady and Lane, 1996; Fillis, 2007). Those owner/managers from a non-Irish background export to a wider selection of markets; for example English craftspeople export to Japan, Singapore, the Middle East and South Africa in addition to Europe and North America.

Knott (1994) estimated that the economic contribution of the sector in England, Scotland and Wales was £400m. In the past decade in the United Kingdom a number of surveys have examined the socio-economic impact of craft, including craft practitioners' future hopes in developing their work. McAuley and Fillis (2002) estimated that the sector turnover in Scotland was £151m with nearly three quarters wishing to expand their practice. McAuley and Fillis (2004) also estimated that the turnover for English and Welsh makers was £826m, with an almost similar proportion wishing to grow their work. McAuley and Fillis (2006) estimate that a total sectoral turnover of around £26m is possible within Northern Ireland. So it seems reasonable to suggest that craft has much more to offer in economic and creative senses.

Using the Data to Construct a Craft Typology

By drawing on the qualitative results in conjunction with the quantitative survey findings, a profile of the owners of craft enterprises can be constructed. The triangulation process allows for a deeper interpretation of the data than if a single methodological approach had been used.

Motivational issues

Since a large percentage of the craft enterprises investigated in this research consists of a single worker/manager, motivational problems can play a significant role in the development of the craft business, as the following interview extract illustrates:

> Sometimes I think it's so bad, I'm going to give up and do a different job –
> other times I think I'm definitely going to carry on but change everything.

Makers can overcome motivational problems by creating a workshop or cooperative environment. Small numbers of people producing together, but not necessarily manufacturing the same type of work, can stimulate one another in terms of both creative and business ideas.

Philosophical clashes – product versus market orientation

The belief that the craft is produced for its own sake, without any market influence, is held by a number of respondents. They tend to view themselves more as artists or designers rather than craftspeople. This type of producer does not feel comfortable with the term 'product' and tends to believe, instead, in making objects which he/she has feelings for. This then introduces certain sensory or aesthetic dimensions into the process of making and selling. By following their own creative instincts and by not responding to market demand they believe they will not lose touch with the product through their refusal to compromise; as one individual commented:

> I wouldn't really call it a product because people usually associate that with a function.
> It would be one-off pieces, one-off works. I try not to use the word.

Those with negative attitudes towards business and marketing concepts tend to construct barriers against any attempts to move them towards customer orientation. One respondent remarked:

> I don't really like selling, basically. I can't stand standing on a trade stand and selling to people.

Another demonstrates the dichotomy which exists:

> The marketing is the difficult bit. There are two ways of approaching this sort of thing – the first is to produce what the market wants, the other is to produce what you want to do. In many respects the doing what you want to do is the prima donna approach, but in many respects that's the gamble you've got to take.

There are risks associated with this approach; many owner/managers are prepared to take risks associated with the product, while others combine both product and market risks. One respondent explained his philosophy:

*I wouldn't go into a production idea with it at all. I think you've got to take risks.
I can't compromise the creative/artistic position with what the public wants.*

Following this creative position can be beneficial but there may also be some problems; a number of respondents remarked that the creative spark is not a constant element and that their business does pass through various phases of inactivity as they run out of steam. In common with many other small businesses, the typical craft enterprise is limited in what it can achieve due to its size and lack of resources.

Marketing/Entrepreneurship interface competencies

Advertising was not an option for many craft enterprises; instead they used a combination of lower cost approaches such as word-of-mouth marketing and trade show attendance in order to construct a reputation over time:

The main method of selling is through word of mouth or people seeing it at the exhibitions. Exhibitions are very important. Advertising is extremely costly and you've to keep up the momentum with that. I think exhibitions are the best ... And it's really just building up the value of your name. Sometimes it's not just a piece of work they buy, it's because it's by so and so.

The techniques of word-of-mouth marketing and networking in the craft sector are also found in the wider SME community. Many respondents perceived that exporting was a secondary activity and were much more reliant on domestic sales, while others became almost immediately involved in international activity. The main selling methods used were craft fair attendance and selling via retailers. The trade fair tended to be used both by those embarking on a career in the crafts and also by those who have been working in the sector for some time. Benefits included the ability to make contact with other makers and buyers from both the domestic and overseas markets. One believed that:

the formation of relationships/networking is really important - you meet a lot of people at craft fairs who turn into good friends or good contacts.

This leads to the adoption of a networking approach to carrying out their craft practice and business generally, it can be useful in the early stages of development in order to gain access to information on selling in the domestic market and also with gaining access to export markets. This approach is also adopted at major international trade fairs:

I did Chelsea for the first time and this American buyer came along and ordered quite a lot of work from me. And it's just built up from there ...

Once I got into Chelsea, that's when all the offers came up for me to go to San Francisco and New York.

The results have uncovered a range of attitudes with implications for behaviour in both domestic and export markets. Differences in orientation have direct consequences for issues relating to decision making, with owner/manager philosophy often dominating over external influences.

The data have shown that there are a variety of beliefs, attitudes, behaviours and orientations being exhibited across the sector (Table 1). Triangulation has resulted in the interpretative construction of four orientations of people working with craft (Silverman, 1994).

Previous profiling attempts in other industry sectors have tended to result in the production of an either/or scenario with little effort to go beyond the proactive/reactive or aggressive/passive level of understanding of organisation and owner/manager orientation (Cavusgil, 1984). Excerpts from the qualitative interviews are used here to illustrate each orientation. There are those who have chosen to work in the industry because of the importance of the lifestyle quality involved and are unwilling to sacrifice this in order to expand the business – 'the lifestyler'. Growth beyond a certain point means unwanted additional commitments:

> *If we were to move on, it would be by substantially changing the products, but adhering to the same sort of market and at the same sort of level. And the possibility if we bumped into the right sort of person, employing somebody who fitted in precisely with what we did. Then we could clearly double our throughput possibly, which would be a big boost to the business, if looked upon as a business. We tend not to look upon it as a business – it's a way of life and it is a business because that's the best way to fit in with income tax and all the rest.*

Another type of individual is the business-oriented entrepreneur who is willing to take risks and recognises the importance of developing a customer base – 'the entrepreneur'. Networking and relationship building are deemed very important for success. The craft object tends not to be viewed as art but as a commercial product. The owner of this form of craft enterprise exhibits ambition for growth and, although he/she may sometimes view formal marketing techniques negatively, the more creative form of entrepreneurial marketing is embraced in order to generate profits:

> *I'd like very much to go abroad. Marketing you're stuck with. I don't like anything to do with marketing – it's an absolute pain but it is unavoidable and it does have to be addressed. And that's why, when I moved from being a sole trader, and quite purposefully one of the three of us spends the entire time marketing and I spend maybe 20% of my entire time marketing, maybe more. That's a big investment. And we have to do it. I specifically got involved with other people in order that I didn't have to do it myself, because I don't like it, I'm not good at it. I'm very cynical about it. What we do is craft in that it contains that ethos but it's not craft like what most people regard craft as – we make practical things for private people, we produce furniture for local authorities, we furnish auditoriums. The reference points are very, very close to craft but in many respects it's a product.*

The third form can be described as an artist/designer who is unwilling to view craft as a product but rather as a creative object – 'the idealist'. Their stance is uncompromising when producing the work. They do not tend to take note of customer demand but instead make art/craft which they feel has artistic integrity. In other words, they embrace an Art for Art's sake rather than Art for Business sake philosophy (Harrison *et al*, 1998). This is not to say that they do not exhibit certain recognised entrepreneurial characteristics in that they do take risks as far as the work is concerned in order to break new ground. They can be innovative and certainly creative:

> *Convincing people of the worth of it, the value of it … (is) the main issue, because it falls between the arts and a craft. I started off as a craftsperson, making quilts. As I became more involved in my work the quilters wouldn't accept them. Because I went beyond the boundaries of what was acceptable within the craft. So I only exhibit now in art galleries and do commissions as works of art. I don't do any utilitarian things now.*

There is a fourth type who may enter the industry much later than the other groups; they tend to have gained previous work experience in unrelated areas and have decided to make a career change – 'the late developer'. Depending on their background, a number of key skills can be brought into the new venture but the importance of lifestyle quality appears to be significant here too. This has relevance for expansion in terms of sales, markets and numbers being employed in the enterprise:

Several characteristics can be found in more than one group: for instance, both the entrepreneur and the idealist are prepared to take risks. However, it is the nature of the risk that is inherently different. The former is prepared to indulge in risk taking at the business and product level, while the latter is really only concerned with artistic risk. Being prepared to take risks, having control over the creative direction of craft development, not being afraid to fail and having the perseverance to succeed all contribute to creative output. Many of these factors are central to success not just with respect to craft but also across the smaller enterprise environment generally where owner/managers have set up businesses to serve an inner need to succeed on their own terms.

Conclusion

Many craft enterprises engage in international activities, helped in part by their competency portfolio. Severe resource constraints are overcome through the development of artistic product and business-related competencies grounded in creativity and innovation. Those working in the craft sector can be viewed as an example of successful entrepreneurial marketing practice in organisations operating on very limited budgets; they are able to differentiate themselves in the marketplace and achieve competitive advantage through application of creativity of both thought and practice. If creativity is viewed as rejection of established modes of practice in favour of alternative methods, then the lifestyler is creative in following a philosophy where quality of existence is much more important than business expansion and profit making. The entrepreneur embraces creativity in the approach to business and in the design of the product. The idealist utilises creative, artistic practice in the making of the craft object, relying on reputation rather than business and marketing skills in order to secure sales of the work. The late developer has been creative in terms of making the decision to switch vocations and in the ability to apply experience gained in other industry sectors.

LIFESTYLER	ENTREPRENEUR
Expansion of business unimportant	Risk taker most likely to embrace business and marketing philosophy Long-term realisation of importance of customer relationships/networking
Unwilling to take many risks	Mixture of intrinsic and extrinsic motivation effects
Importance of quality of life	Mixed aesthetics of business and artistic priorities
May or may not export	Creative approaches to production and marketing
Generally reactive	Opportunity driven
Unwilling to follow business and marketing philosophy and develop related skills	Use of entrepreneurial marketing competencies
Strong use of the lifestyle aesthetic	Motivated by profit
Creative approach to making craft	Most likely to grow the business
Motivated by quality of life	Best chance of exporting the work due to entrepreneurial drive
Will expand based on comfortable level	
IDEALIST	**LATE DEVELOPER**
Risk taker with the craft	Tends to come from non-creative background
Unwilling to accept business and marketing philosophy	Less likely to export
Dominance of 'Art for Art's sake' beliefs	Unlikely to accept 'new' ideas
May or may not export	Believes in valuing own experience of business and life
Realisation of importance of establishing and building relationships and generating reputation	Able to bring outside skills to the business (*eg* sales and marketing)
Views self as artist rather than craftsperson	May find problems with accessing existing networks
Motivated by connection with art	Motivated by being able to pursue alternative career path
Will have concerns over mass production	May or may not grow production depending on comfort level
Intrinsically motivated	May be slow to find effective blend of business and creative synergy endeavours
Uses high levels of creativity to make craft as art	
Strong use of artistic competencies	
Heightened impact of aesthetics as art	

Table 1. A Craft Typology

Further Reading

Anderson, D.R., Sweeney, D.J. and Williams, T.A. (1996) *Statistics for Business and Economics.*
USA, West Publishing Company.

Aslin, E. (1981) *The Aesthetic Movement – Prelude to Art Nouveau.* London, Ferndale Editions.

Bell, J., Crick, D. and Young, S. (2004) Small firm internationalization and business strategy: an exploratory
study of 'knowledge intensive' and 'traditional' manufacturing firms in the UK. *International Small Business Journal,*
22 (1), 23–56.

Bilkey, W.J. (1982) Variables Associated with Export Profitability. **Journal of International Business Studies,** 13, 39–55.

Bruce, A. and Filmer, P. (1983) *Working in Crafts – An Independent Socio-Economic Study of Craftsmen and Women
in England and Wales.* London, Crafts Council.

Bryman, A. and Cramer, D. (1997) *Quantitative Data Analysis with SPSS for Windows: A Guide for Social Scientists.*
London, Routledge.

Carson, D., Cromie, S., McGowan, P. and Hill, J. (1995) *Marketing and Entrepreneurship in SMEs. An Innovative Approach.*
UK, Prentice Hall.

Cavusgil, S.T. (1984) Differences Among Exporting Firms based on their Degree of Internationalisation.
Journal of Business Research, 12, 195–208.

Collaborative Economics (2001) *The Creative Community: Leveraging Creativity and Cultural Participation for Silicon
Valley's Economic and Civic Future.* Working Paper. San Jose, Cultural Initiatives Silicon Valley.

Collinson, E. and Shaw, E. (2001) Entrepreneurial marketing – a historical perspective on development and practice.
Management Decision, 39 (9), 761–766.

Coopers & Lybrand (firm) (1994) *The Employment and Economic Significance of the Cultural Industries in Ireland.*
Dublin, Coopers & Lybrand.

Department for Business Innovation and Skills (2009) *Small and Medium Enterprise Statistics for the UK and Regions.*
[Online] Available from http://stats.bis.gov.uk/ed/sme/ [Accessed 11th February 2010].

Department of Trade and Industry (2002) *Small and Medium Enterprise (SME) Statistics for the UK 2001.*

Dormer, P. (1997) The Salon de Refuse? In Dormer P. (ed.) *The Culture of Craft: Status and Future.*
Manchester, Manchester University Press.

Fielden, S.L., Davidson, M.J. and Makin, P.J. (2000) Barriers Encountered During Micro and Small Business Start-Up
in North-West England. *Journal of Small Business and Enterprise Development,* 7 (4), 295–304.

Fillis, I. (2000). An Examination of the Internationalisation Process of the Smaller Craft Firm in the United Kingdom
and the Republic of Ireland. [unpublished doctoral thesis]. University of Stirling.

Fillis, I. (2002a) Creative Craft Behaviour in Britain and Ireland. *Irish Marketing Review,* 15 (1), 38–48.

Fillis, I. (2002b) Barriers to Internationalisation: An Investigation of the Craft Microenterprise.
European Journal of Marketing, 36 (7/8), 912–927.

Fillis, I. (2002c) The Internationalisation Process of the Craft Firm Microenterprise. *Journal of Developmental
Entrepreneurship,* 7 (1), 25–43.

Fillis, I. (2002d) An Andalusian dog or a rising star: creativity and the marketing/entrepreneurship interface.
Journal of Marketing Management, 18 (3/4), 379–395.

Fillis, I. (2003) Image, Reputation and Identity Issues in the Arts and Crafts Organisation. *Corporate Reputation Review:
An International Journal,* 6 (3), 239–251.

Fillis, I. (2004) The Internationalising Smaller Craft Firm: Insights from the Marketing and Entrepreneurship Interface.
International Small Business Journal, 22 (1), 57–82.

Fillis, I. (2007) Celtic Craft and the Creative Consciousness as Contributions to Marketing Creativity. *Journal of Strategic Marketing,* 15 (1), 7–16.

Fillis, I. (2008) The Internationalisation Process of the Smaller Firm: An Examination of the Craft Microenterprise. *The Open Business Journal,* 1, 53–61.

Forbes, E. and Munro, D. (1988) *The Scottish Development Agency: An Example to the Nation?* London, Tory Reform Group.

Gill, J. and Johnson, P. (1991) *Research Methods for Managers.* London, Paul Chapman Publishing Ltd.

Gray, A. and McGuigan, J. (1993) *Studying Culture: An Introductory Reader.* London, Edward Arnold.

Hamill, J. and Gregory, K. (1997) Internet Marketing in the Internationalisation of UK SMEs. Journal of Marketing Management, 13, 9–28.

Harrison, C., Wood, P. and Gaiger, J. (1998) Art in Theory 1815–1900: An Anthology of Changing Ideas. Oxford, Blackwell Publishers.

Hart, S, Webb, J.R and Jones, M.V. (1994) Export Marketing Research and the Effect of Export Experience in Industrial SMEs. *International Marketing Review,* 11 (6), 4–22.

Healy, K. (2002) What's New for Culture in the New Economy? *Journal of Arts Management Law and Society,* 32 (2), 86–103.

Heslop, T.A. (1997) How Strange the Change from Major to Minor: Hierarchies and Medieval Art. In Dormer P. (ed.) *The Culture of Craft: Status and Future.* Manchester, Manchester University Press.

Hesmondhalgh, D. (2002) *The Cultural Industries.* London, Sage.

Johanson, J. and Mattsson, L-G. (1988) Internationalisation in Industrial Systems – A Network Approach. In Hood N. and Vahlne J-E. (eds.) Strategies in Global Competition. USA, The Stockholm School of Economics, Croom Helm.

Johanson, J. and Vahlne, J-E. (1977) The Internationalization Process of a Firm: A Model of Knowledge Development and Increasing Foreign Market Commitments. Journal of International Business Studies, 8, 23–32.

Keeble, D., Lawson, C., Smith, H.L., Moore, B. and Wilkinson, F. (2004) Internationalisation Processes, Networking and Local Embeddedness in Technology-Intensive Small Firms. *Small Business Economics,* 11 (4), 327–342.

Kidder, L.H. and Judd, C.M. (1986) *Research Methods in Social Relations.* London, Holt Rinehart and Winston.

Knight, G. and Cavusgil, S.T. (2004) Innovation, organizational capabilities and the born global firm. *Journal of International Business Studies,* 35 (2), 124–141.

Knott, C.A. (1994) *Crafts in the 1990s: a socio-economic study of craftspeople in England, Scotland and Wales.* London, Crafts Council.

Kolbe, R.H. and Burnett, M.S. (1991) Content-Analysis Research: an examination of applications with directives for improving research reliability and objectivity. *Journal of Consumer Research,* 18 (2), 243–251.

Leeke, D. (1994) *Audit of the Craft Sector in Northern Ireland,* report completed for Craftworks NI (Ltd).

McAuley, A. and Fillis, I. (2002) *Crafts businesses in Scotland: a study.* Report for the Scottish Arts Council, Scottish Enterprise and Scottish Enterprise Glasgow, Glasgow.

McAuley, A. and Fillis, I. (2004) *Making it in the Twenty-first Century: a socio-economic study of craftspeople in England and Wales 2003/2004.* Report for Crafts Council and Arts Councils of England and Wales, London.

McAuley, A. and Fillis, I. (2006) *A Future in the Making: a socio-economic study of makers in Northern Ireland.* Report for Craft Northern Ireland, Belfast.

Matlay, H. (2004) E-entrepreneurship and small e-business development: towards a comparative research agenda. *Journal of Small Business and Enterprise Development,* 11 (3), 408–414.

Metcalf, B. (1997) Craft and Art, Culture and Biology. In Dormer P. (ed.) *The Culture of Craft: status and future.* Manchester, Manchester University Press.

Myerscough, J. (1996) *The Arts and the Northern Ireland Economy.* Belfast, Northern Ireland Economic Council.

Naylor, G. (1971) *The Arts and Crafts Movement.* Great Britain, Studio Vista.

O'Grady, S. and Lane, H.W. (1996) The Psychic Distance Paradox. *Journal of International Business Studies,* 27 (2), 309–321.

Oppenheim, A.N. (1992) *Questionnaire Design, Interviewing and Attitude Measurement.* London, Pinter Publishers.

Rialp, A., Rialp, J. and Knight, G.A. (2005) The Phenomenon of Early Internationalizing Firms: what do we know after a decade (1993–2003) of scientific enquiry? *International Business Review,* 14 (2), 147–166.

Silverman, D. (1994) *Interpreting Qualitative Data: methods for analysing talk, text and interaction.* London, Sage.

Welch, E. (1997) *Art and Society in Italy 1350–1500.* Oxford, Oxford University Press.

The Making: value and values in the craft object

Martin Woolley

Contemporary crafts in the UK occupy an ill-defined position within modern material culture, and would benefit from greater clarity in terms of: where they fit, how their value system operates and their relationship with consumer culture. This contribution to the debate is around key themes – examining the strengths and weaknesses of contemporary crafts; secondly, defining the values associated with craft objects and thirdly, identifying how these 'values' are/are not, communicated to a wider public. By increasing an informed understanding of the meaning and significance of crafts, opportunities for wider practice and improved 'marketing' may create a more sustainable market and craft profession.

The aims which Crouch and Barnes (2001) list in *'A Brief History of the Keswick School of Industrial Art'* relate to points made later about the human values and connections engendered to both makers, and the well-being of society, of craft products:

> *The early years of the school saw a list of rules established which carried on well into the modern period. The aims of the KSIA were stated as such:*
>
> 1. *To counteract the pernicious effects of turning men into machines without the possibility of love for their work.*
>
> 2. *To make it felt that hand-work really does allow expression of a man's soul and self, and so is worth doing for its own sake, and worth purchasing even at some cost to the buyer.*
>
> 3. *To try to displace by hand-work the crude metal and wooden ornaments produced by steel dies and hydraulic presses.*
>
> 4. *To show that here in England an abundance of skill of hand is wasted which, if any education worth its name were given to the whole working man – to his eye, hand, heart, as well as head – could and would help England. (p. 2)*

Positioning contemporary UK crafts

Discussion of contemporary crafts is hampered by the inherent difficulties involved in determining the junction between the 'contemporary' and the 'traditional', given that the former frequently draws on the latter for technique and design influence. In reality, this is a graded rather than fixed comparative in which the bulk of craft activity takes place in-between the two extremes. Accompanying this bipolar 'analogue' relationship is a subtle change in terminology, with 'craftsman' associated with traditional practice, 'craftsperson' associated with the contemporary crafts as practised since the gender-equality period of the 1970s and design 'makers', or 'crafter' identifying a more radical form of practice, which directly challenges the previous two exemplars, in a 'knitting-with-attitude' stance. This latter development aligns with popular or street culture values, making inroads into the elitist, soft, 'safe' values of the traditional and contemporary craft markets.

History: Vaizey (2007) argues that the positive status of the handmade is firmly established as a conscious counterpoint to mass manufacture. The idealisation of the hand-made object began – understandably if simplistically – during the Industrial Revolution. In the West, since the invention of mass production, the hand-made has inexorably become more expensive, and a status symbol'. The notion of 'idealisation' is useful here as, contemporaneous with the romantic view of bygone rural traditions; it represents an edited view of traditional crafts in which stultifying labour, exploitation and harsh working practices have been erased. So successful has this been, that professional contemporary craft practice is viewed as an ideal work–life model in which labour is viewed as fulfilling, developmental, expressive and creative, an ethos symbolically transferred to a select public, who purchase to buy into this ethos, via the craft objects themselves.

It is important to avoid oversimplification in defining current craft activities by assuming that 'contemporary crafts' are the only meaningful current craft activities. More realistically, Figure 1 illustrates the diversity of current craft activities, which vary from the skilful reproduction found in 'modern antiques', through 'handmade' goods batch produced for export by developing countries, to the spectrum of contemporary craft activities: which varies from simple functionality of ceramic tableware to the contrasting status of fine art works with a craft ethos. Haute couture is an example, where one-off uniqueness is celebrated at extreme prices – the choice of expensive materials, attention to detail and finish, are aligned with time-consuming, hand-executed techniques, the garments attaining the status of artworks in the process. It is worth noting the perceived 'decadence' of haute couture, in contrast with the posited humanitarian values associated with handmade work in other design/art areas; fine art status and values neatly avoid the perception of overindulgent consumerism. However fashions change, the secretive elite market of wealthy supporter/purchasers of couture is shrinking, the consequence is a dying/reducing skill-base: couture atelier craft worker numbers have fallen from 46,000 in the 1950s to 4000 today ('The Secret World of Haute Couture', 2007), where a few wealthy patrons are supporting and thereby preserving and protecting the specialist craft skills of the couture workshops.

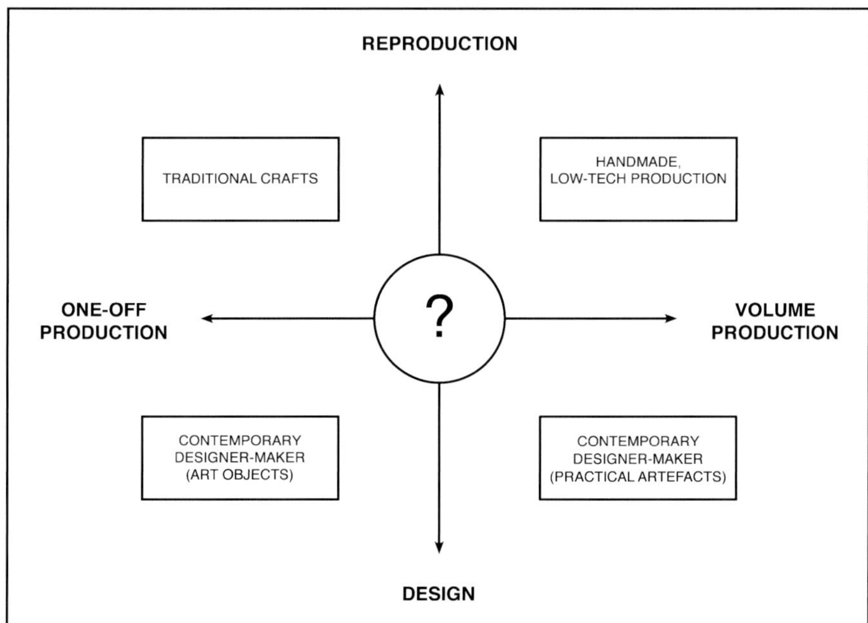

Figure 1. The range of craft activities

Placement: The polarised view of the crafts is blurred by overlaps between the quadrants. Thus the contemporary designer-maker may draw on traditional techniques; the traditional craftsperson may create both one-offs whilst also engaging in batch production. This blurring of boundaries began post-war; Frayling in Pye *et al* (1986) describes the relatively complex position in the mid-1980s:

> there is the complexity of today's craft scene, where the work of makers from the three main traditions of craft activity in the twentieth century – the Arts and Crafts tradition, the Council of Industrial Design tradition and, most recently, the 'craftsman's art' tradition – all go under the general (if misleading) title of 'the crafts': some of these makers are highly mindful of the traditions to which they belong, other are slightly embarrassed about them, and others try to isolate themselves entirely. This has made it extremely difficult to place today's craftwork in a longer-term perspective. (Foreword; p.10)

The primary focus of this paper is on the contemporary UK craft movement, defined as a branch of the crafts that has its origins and influences positioned within the mainstream art/design college sector and contemporary gallery/exhibition/retail system; where designer-makers embody the collective debates and 'aesthetic values' common in these closely related educational and cultural systems. It is difficult for most makers to survive economically through practice alone, and so there is often a symbiotic relationship between the two, with higher education providing steady supplementary income, alongside the less predictable craft income. Indeed, this fusion of income streams is personified by funding models such as the Arts and Humanities Research Council Research Leave scheme which funds academics to carry out practice-based research and conversely, Fellowships in the Creative and Performing Arts, which assists practitioners to pursue their work within the higher education (HE) environment. It can be argued that this proximity is primarily responsible for the unique fusion in the UK of idealistic values and practice; degree level courses, or their equivalents, are duty bound to incorporate an understanding of history, cultural context and values, alongside the practicalities of making skills and knowledge.

The economic context of contemporary crafts in the UK is further affected by the historic division between artists and makers, whereby a sculpture should cost substantially more than a pot, because making useful objects has connotations of 'trade', an area frowned upon by the middle classes in the nineteenth century which perpetuates today. This division, between art artefacts and makers' products is reflected through the UK agencies that support and fund artists and arts organisations notably the Arts Councils of England ‹http://www.artscouncil.org.uk›, Scotland ‹http://www.scottisharts.org.uk› and Northern Ireland ‹http://www.artscouncil-ni.org›. These agencies are always in a state of flux reviewing their terms of reference and changing their patterns of support (Jones, 2007c; Thomas, 2007), a current change being Creative Scotland (Jones, 2007a,b; The Scottish Government, 2010). Makers are supported through the Crafts Council (2010):

> the UK's national organisation for the promotion of contemporary crafts. Established in 1971, they are an independent body funded by the Arts Council of England, responsible for promoting fine craftsmanship, encouraging high standards and increasing public awareness of contemporary crafts and applied arts. (Craftscotland, 2010)

The counterbalance of support is from the UK Government's Department for Business, Innovation and Skills (BIS) ‹ http://www.bis.gov.uk/›.

Relationship with intelligent technologies: The position of technology to the crafts has been seriously debated and generally centres on the validity, or otherwise, of employing technologies that are perceived as intervening between the physical presence of the maker and the object, as Aldersey-Williams (2007: 36–41) suggests 'A tool or technology always distances maker from object. At the heart of the present debate is how great that distance can become'. A significant issue today for designer-makers is their relationship with the intelligent technological tools that are increasingly available. Sophisticated tools which support, influence and inspire prototypes, initiating and facilitating the making of new, unique craft forms which were not possible in the last millennium, are increasingly celebrated. These include developments in microscopy which have inspired and been translated into some formidable work. Discussions circle around whether such facilities dilute the product outcomes as 'craft' objects or merely extend the craft ethos in a new direction.

> *Interface (exhibition) makes a persuasive case that craft is not about hand-held or 'primitive' technology. What seems to be more important for these makers is the materials that are used rather than the technologies by which they are worked. (Aldersey-Williams, 2007: 39)*

On another level, creating sales, technology also makes possible micro manufacture at the point of sale; such as: when a client purchases a chair 'the material is ordered, measured and cut … can be made fast enough to enable a crafted product to compete with mass manufacture' (Aldersey-Williams, 2007: 39). Thus the practical value of new technologies can lie in both the positive attribute of original experimentation, through the creative exploration of new potentials with original results and production/design efficiencies. Whereas the corresponding effect on values can lie equally in a negative view of technology dehumanising the innate qualities of the crafts.

The cost of skill: Another criterion that could have been used to identify crafted products in the past was the number of items created within a single production batch, which often related to technological support. The general rule being: that there is a diminishing value as the volume of production increases. Thus a 'unique' one-off piece will command an optimum price; at the other end of the scale, high volume, 'hand-finished' products will be of lower value. There are exceptions, usually related to a specific production context, for example the role of the kiln in handcrafted ceramics is volume production in relation to an energy and labour efficient technology; crucially the kiln does not replace nor diminish hand processes. Thus, craft values in ceramics remain unchallenged, whereas technological intervention at the pre-kiln 'creative' stages might well be viewed in a different light.

Since the high value placed on an item is often because each one takes time to make, the appropriate level of return for the effort made in the making of a product, crafts are displayed for purchase in precious environments, for example in galleries and exclusive boutiques which have significant costs, with a consequent high mark-up. For these reasons the crafted item has become associated with high cost and exclusiveness, which limits the market. Purchasers tend to be an appreciative elite, although paradoxically their reasons for acquiring the craft product may be because they associate such a purchase with the retro-values of 'integrity and social responsibility … a return to simplicity, honesty and beauty' (Kelley, 2001).

Mainstream material culture and markets: Contemporary craft products have had a pervasive influence on mainstream areas of material culture: interior design, fashion, architecture and product design have been informed by craft influences to both personalise and humanise designs; to move beyond the predictable, narrow machine aesthetic to embrace more varied and complex finishes, materials and forms. David Mellor's hand-finished, machine-made cutlery produced in his model factory represents a transitional example (Mellor, 2010).

> *David Mellor's approach to design has been to some extent that of the craftsman, in the way he has focused on the effective use of materials and making techniques and his insistence on the highest standards of environment and working conditions for himself and his employees.*
> *(Loughborough University, 2006)*

A more overtly commercial deployment of the 'craft look' is Marks & Spencer 'Per Una' and 'Autograph' middle-cost fashion ranges, with machine produced hand-knitted looks and machine-'crafted' individual buttons, the garments are on the rails in small numbers, implying only a few items available, however, identical garment ranges are in every store across the country and promoted through online shopping (Marks and Spencer Group plc, 2010). This influence goes beyond aesthetic pastiche into areas more commonly associated with 'craft values' in tandem with advanced production technology. In Table 1 this interplay between the values inherent in the craft object with those associated with mass-produced

	CRAFT OBJECTS	**MASS-PRODUCED OBJECTS**
OBJECTS	Embody the 'hand of the creator'	Embody the precision of the machine
	Directly embody the manifestations of skill and creativity	Indirectly embody the skill and creativity of the design, production and marketing system
	Longevity a priority	Built-in obsolescence
	Positioned within a wider (historical, societal and craft) cultural context	Positioned within a wider (historical, societal and craft) cultural context
	Associated with originality	Associated with innovation
	Limited formal 'functionality'	Predicated on 'functionality'
	Limited range of object archetypes	Wide range of object archetypes
PRACTITIONER/ PRODUCER	Goals related to personal and professional development	Goals related to organisational growth and profitability
	Project personal values	Project corporate values
	Designer-maker continuum	Designer-producer schism
	Located within a developing body of personal work	Located within a developing product/service range and/or brand
MARKET	Specialist market	Non-specialist markets
	Narrow-cast advertising and promotion	Mass marketing and advertising

Table 1. Comparison of craft and mass-produced object characteristics

objects can be examined for commonalities and differences to understand their respective contexts. Cross-fertilisation of values can also be found where the inspiration and qualities of fine art are adapted by designers and vice versa; so too are the qualities of the crafted item when transferred/translated into manufacturing processes to imitate a hand-finish quality in products. This is seen particularly in the fashion industry where age-old manual techniques for buttons, embroidery, beaded work and jewellery are given a patina of hand craftsmanship, implying that each item is superficially unique, even when made entirely by intelligent machines at any requisite volume. In effect, clever copies or pastiche objects are mass-produced because they are familiar and will sell in greater quantities, in preference to creating original works/garments using new materials and processes. However there are examples where there is a synergy between craft and manufacture, between creativity and new materials, as in the recent government funded HE research project 'The Emotional Wardrobe' whose aim is

*... to explore how the value of clothing and fashion can be extended through the integration
of information and communication functions, informed by and informing new technological
developments, and building on the traditional concepts of clothing and associated cultures
as expressive and communicative medium that connects the body with our social world.
(The Emotional Wardrobe, 2006)*

These emerging values engendered by the integration of craft with disruptive technologies
are in marked contrast to the more traditional craft values associated with high quality. As for
example exemplified by Pye's view from a 1960's perspective (1968):

*The crafts are a border-ground of manufacturing industry, and nearly every object they make has
its counterpart and competitor in something manufactured for the same purpose. In all but a very
few trades exceedingly high quality is the last remaining ground on which the crafts can now
compete. (p. 133)*

Eco-efficiency: Allied to the intrinsic beauty of the design and form of a craft object is
the economic use of materials. McDonough and Braungart (2002) qualify the principle of
eco-efficiency:

*Primarily the term means 'doing more with less', a precept which has its roots in early
industrialisation. Henry Ford was adamant about lean and clean operating policies ...
You must get the most out of the power, out of the material, and out of the time.*

Makers exemplify McDonough and Braungart's position on eco-effectiveness that,
rather than recycling, products should be created with 'downcycling' as a principle
automatically considered by makers, not Cradle to Grave but 'Cradle to Cradle'. In other words
employing relatively benign processes and materials to produce objects that are timeless,
passed on from one generation to another, craft objects can be considered to be sustainable
in environmental terms. The principle of 'affective sustainability' of objects as defined by
Borjessen (2007) in a recently completed doctoral study, can be applied to craft objects.

Limitations in Current Understanding

'In the know': Contemporary crafts are often located within a self-referential culture of
a small international cognoscente. It is tempting to assume that niche consumers are fully
cognisant of the values, methods and contexts of contemporary crafts, enabling them to
make informed decisions about their purchases which attain meaningful absorption into
their lives. In terms of the available 'hard' practical information, this is probably true, thanks
to the Internet, style magazines, television and the media, the crafts are better publicised
than they were and are more accessible. However, such sources rarely communicate the 'soft
information' central to the craft ideology and aesthetic. In particular it is relatively difficult to
accurately communicate the sensory experience that handling craft objects engender. This
'soft' information is rooted in the real-world immediacy of the object itself and includes:

- Directly experienced sensory qualities – tactile, sound, smell, weight and taste

- Process qualities communicated directly from the practitioner to the customer
  though public access to the studio or workshop

- Specific visual qualities that can only be effectively communicated directly:
  transparency, translucency, reflection, colour, finish and the impact of different
  lighting conditions.

It could be argued that the advent of virtual communication has diminished the opportunities to engage with the subtleties of soft information through the object itself. The maker is increasingly utilising the worldwide web to create a surrogate impression because it is cheaper, more effective and more efficient to market themselves and their artefacts to a wider customer base. Equally, it may be the case that as the Internet makes craft activities and their location better known, it also creates more opportunities for real world access and engagement with the soft information provided by real artefacts. Crafts represent an antidote to the global market; they are, to a degree, resistant to virtual marketing relying frequently on local retail outlets. Latterly, blogging has lent a radical dimension to craft activity, engendering new, challenging debates, manifestos and approaches to the crafts, which reflect views beyond the traditional educational and practitioner groups commonly dominating debate. Although related, the values associated with the craft object are different from their inherent value as communicated in soft information. 'We present craft and design to a wide range of audiences and promote craft values through exhibitions, our retail space, public programs and publications' (Craft Victoria, 2010). Some significant craft values listed below are the antithesis of the value associated with mass production. Whilst the former reflect the 'genuine' values of the practitioner, inevitably the latter reflect 'manufactured' corporate values. Craft values are variable, frequently based on the wide-ranging philosophies of individual practitioners; the following represent some common generic examples:

- Aesthetic vision and personality of the practitioner

- Explicit creativity and originality

- Qualities of workmanship and demonstrable skill

- Integrity and consistency of approach – truth to materials

- The preservation of traditional techniques, qualities and contexts

- Wide-ranging ethics in relation to work, the environment and the natural order

- Self sufficiency

- The rural and/or local

- Internationalism – an international view in contrast to globalisation.

This list represents ethical production with the relationship between the practitioner and the customer being a subtle interplay of values. Ultimately the artefact could be seen as a viable and transferable symbol of such a value system. In gently subverting the mass production system, consciously or otherwise, the crafts inhabit a 'comfortable counter-culture' representing alternatives rather than suggestions.

> *for someone who is less interested than Ely in legitimating judicial review by distinguishing it from legislation, and is more interested in asking questions about how legitimation actually occurs, one learns a great deal from the analogy about how seemingly 'objective' standards or craft values are constantly altering themselves. (Levinson and Balkin, 1991)*

Although this quote relates to music making, it provides an insight into a changing/ evolving world that creates an environment that stimulates change. Unlike traditional crafts, contemporary crafts are seen to have shifting values augmented by debate, soft and hard information in both virtual and real world environments.

As discussed, in the UK there are 'values' implicit in craft objects. The perceived value in relation to the selling price of objects has always been fluid, particularly in craft: when the unique selling point (USP) of the craft product is a 'one-off' creation by an individual, and is increasingly so, since the Industrial Revolution introduced insurmountable competition through mass production. To make a living, and to facilitate the making of further items, the craft practitioner has to provide a convincing package of tangible (material) and intangible (cerebral) values. As Dormer (1997: 228) suggests:

> There are many people producing 'craft' who do not place the emphasis upon making.
> Their emphasis is upon ideas that have an existence that, they say, is separate from
> and not dependent upon making.

'Tangible values' are straightforward, easy to define and verify. They are effortlessly absorbed by the wider public, are transparent and in some cases measurable. In contrast, 'Intangible values' tend to be difficult to define, rely upon the specialist knowledge of a restricted audience and are open to interpretation. Table 2 explores the relationship between two factors: the practical tangible values of craft objects that are usually apparent to a wide public and the intangible values they engender for the more specialist craft market.

TANGIBLE ADDED VALUE	RESULTING INTANGIBLE VALUES
Quality or preciousness of materials and finishes	Luxury
Longevity	Timelessness
Rarity	Uniqueness and originality
Creative reputation of the practitioner	Artistry
Part of a wider body of work or collection	Depth and continuity of the creative vision
Discernable process and making skills	Mastery
Embodied traditions	Historical significance

Table 2. Relationship between tangible and intangible values

The maker generally takes decisions about tangible values as part of the design process; in contrast, intangible values can be manipulated as part of marketing, promotion and their personal identity, artistic vision and craft philosophy. These values can be understood through a range of indicators, notably in the area of skills and mastery and include the following:

- Precision of hand processes

- Complexity, precision, delicacy of work

- Comparative rarity of the process or skill

- Ability to overcome known difficulties in working a material; resistant materials such as oak or diamond often associated with 'risk-taking skills'

- Successful exercising of a known skill communicated through form and/or finish such as wood turning

· Risk-taking to create something new and unique to the maker (Pye, 1986: 53)

· The design concept – shape and form.

In terms of the contemporary market the background knowledge listed as demonstrating the physical skills associated with crafts will be less obvious to the consumer, and if not recognised or understood, such skills will be unappreciated. Most craft processes have a diminishing relationship with contemporary mass production, this means that contemporary hand/eye/tool skills tend to be less well understood compared with earlier periods when there was more personal direct involvement with machines, processes and materials. Today we are more familiar with the output and choice made available through mass manufacture and less familiar with the means of how they are produced. Effectively, unless the consumer has acquired knowledge through a specialised interest and knowledge of production this 'ignorance' poses an increasing dilemma for the crafts, how to communicate the added value of applied skills as they become less familiar, understood or appreciated by the general population. In the future this may mean there will be a diminishing market for designer-maker products.

There is also the duality of crafts associated with 'hobbyist' domestic crafts such as dressmaking, carpentry, knitting, car maintenance; in a previous era when a range of craft processes were undertaken as spare time activities. Whether skilful or not, such activities conditioned a proportion of the population to appreciate the challenges inherent in carrying out fine craftwork, providing an insight into the skills required and the difficulties encountered, which engendered value to work of quality. The range of discerned skills would therefore be higher than it is today.

Risk-taking in performance and the crafts: The concept of risk has been explored by Pye (1986: 53). Nicol (2007) quoting architect Iain Borden argues:

> Allowing for 'risk' presents a huge challenge for those working in public space in a culture where risk aversion is pervasive, that we need to acknowledge and embrace risk in order to create "public space which is always a surprise, a unique place, a stimulation". Borden also posits that "Space that is truly public –acknowledges four kinds of difference. These differences are all about risk-taking, about allowing for the uncertain, unpredictable and not-wholly-programmed to occur." (Nicol, 2007)

Many arts and entertainment activities are forms of discernable risk-taking; often associated with live performance, where real-time risk-taking can be a make or break process, for example theatre and music. Audiences derive pleasure from the tension between the exercising of skill and the possibility of failure. In the case of the circus high wire act, this tension is the primary focus, heightened through dramatic music, lighting, height, timing, the absence (or apparent absence) of safety and stylised body language. In contrast, areas of life where the perception of risk can be reduced by manipulating sensory experience, for example soft music played on planes as they land, to calm passengers at the point at which the flight is perceived to be most dangerous. There is an analogous situation between risk in performance and the applied arts, particularly those which involve right-first-time or irreversible action such as the working of hard, resistant materials or the unique flourish of a glazed brush-stroke. Similarly the value of drawing or sketching is perceived in mark-making as a real-time, one-off event which leaves an indelible, permanent trace. However, such risks can be ameliorated by simply destroying substandard works. In craft terms the risks associated with skill result in either visible risk indicators within the artefact or rely on knowledge by the aficionado that risk-taking has been part of the making process. Such attributes can increase the financial value of the work and the human values it is perceived to embody: reverence for mastery, striving for perfection and dignity of skilled labour.

Chinese brush calligraphy and mark-making within the glaze of Japanese ceramics later adopted by a generation of British potters, notably Bernard Leach inspired by Hamada (Art New Zealand, 2009) personify this attribute. The flourish of the glazed brush stroke is celebrated as much for its sense of real-time skill as it is for its descriptive qualities. To an extent the quality of risk-based skill can be assessed and enjoyed by the observer directly from the craft object, is often described in terms of the visible 'hand of the craftsman' or 'signature' and is integrated into a personal craft style. In contrast, other craft-based objects embody covert skills that cannot be directly discerned from the object, but are understood instead through knowledge of craft processes that do not leave a visible trace (see *Figure 2*).

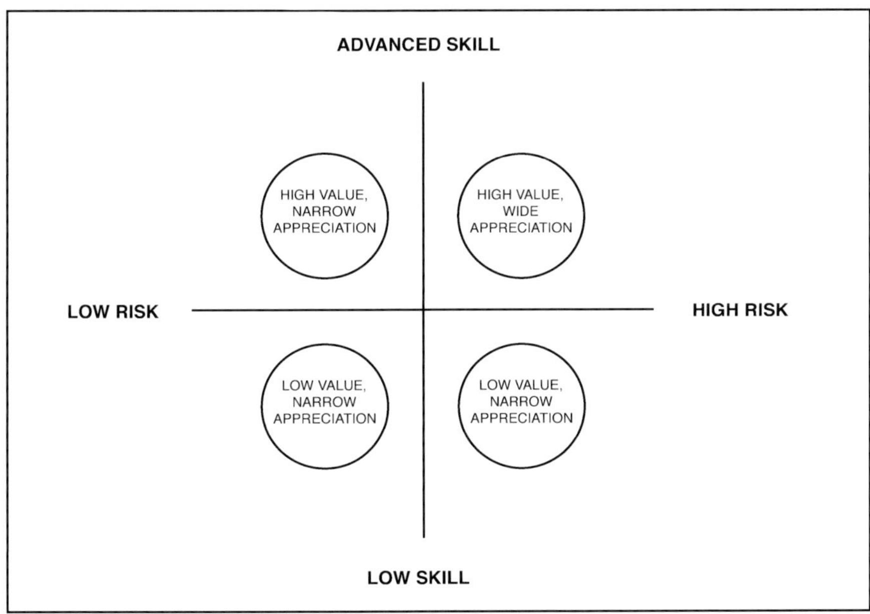

Figure 2 The relationship between skill and risk in the context of perceived value

Skill-based risk in contemporary crafts can take a number of forms, but boils down to one basic premise: the ability to execute a difficult process, or processes, and communicate this directly through the object, or indirectly through knowledgeable and appreciative observers.

The added but unspoken discernible value in craft artefacts is individuality; the value that each artefact is a 'unique' product of human interaction with materials, sharing 'common' values associated with risk and skill.

The Craft Movement and the Mass Market

There has been a general failure of the contemporary craft movement to engage with the 'elusive niches' of the mass market, explained partly in terms of poor communication of value indicators to a wider public. The indicators include the critical issue of discernable skills: the ways craft objects directly communicate and celebrate the skills of the practitioner. Dormer (1997) provides a fundamental clue to the reason behind the lack of communication:

> *a disciplined craft is a body of knowledge with a complex variety of values, and this knowledge is expanded and its values demonstrated and tested, not through language but through practice. It makes craft difficult to write or even talk about with clarity or coherence. (p. 219)*

There has always been a symbiotic relationship, albeit one-way, between crafts and the mass market, whether through overt influences such as high volume craft pastiche or the less obvious use of spurious 'hand-finished' techniques applied to volume production. Compared with the fine art market, there is little which equates with the ways an art work can be 'stretched' to embrace a wider market than just the original, to include: limited edition of identical works, prints; exhibitions, picture loan schemes, artist books, posters, catalogues, recordings, videos, postcards. Three-dimensional craft objects do not lend themselves to market extension as easily as the two-dimensional art object. Again this is because of the primary importance of the craft practitioner's hand as defined by the real object, in contrast with a fine artist's evocation of the conceptual. 'Value' and 'values' are inextricably linked in the original craft piece, in a way that is impossible in copies or other forms of output.

Similarly, low-key marketing of craft works in contrast to mass-market products is assumed to relate to economics, rather than reliance on niche marketing to the cognoscenti through specialist periodicals, shops, galleries, museums and auctions. Interestingly the field of luxury goods often represents a meeting of craft values with mass-market commodities in which the fusion of elitist branding, fashion, preciousness and exclusivity is often wedded to rare and distinctive craft processes.

Niche marketing of craft work depends on communication of the wider craft context through the orthodox channels of mass media and point of sale; it is also reliant on the more specialist methods of exhibition catalogues and siting the means of production alongside a retail space. There are indications that digital media blogs: personal websites, podcasts and online exhibitions are spawning new opportunities for promoting a wider, often more radical, context for the crafts.

Skill Values

According to Frayling (1986):

> *one contributory cause of present confusions of thought about handwork and craftsmanship is perhaps that people have generalised about it who did not know, or did not think enough about, the way tools do actually work. (p. 11)*

The definition of skill in this context is broadened to engage with making and design skills. An overriding value of the craft object is the integration of design with production to form a fused continuum sustained by a unique skill-base, in contrast with the historical dissociation of the two with mass-produced objects. In craft tradition, skill is assumed to be an absolute term, implying an advanced level. In reality, skill, even when associated with successful craft objects, is variable. Figure 3 explores variability of skill levels – the way craft skills run counter to 'deskilling' within wider society with the decline of craft skills in industry and simplification of hand processes in professional trades and DIY. There is little doubt that the rarity of skills associated with craft contributes to perceived value, whilst the integral synergies of design and skill communicate many of the values described.

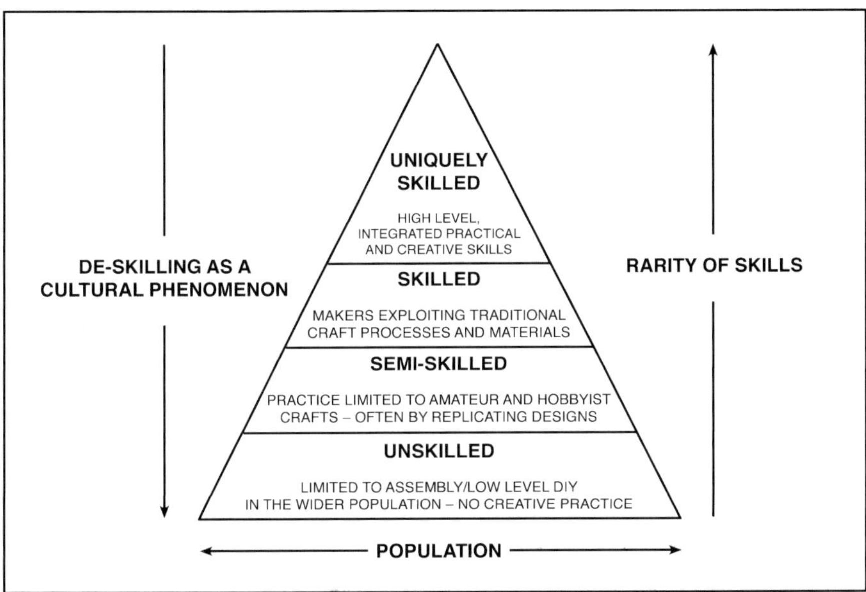

Figure 3. From DIY to studio craft skills – a continuum

The diagram illustrates a subtext in which skills enjoy an increasingly isolated but potentially more valued cultural context. Indeed, it could be argued that part of the contemporary remit of the craft practitioner is to preserve and extend not only traditional skills, but perhaps the entire territory of making skills.

The diagram also represents levels of skill as a continuum rather than as distinct territories. The most relevant interplay is that between 'skilled' and 'uniquely skilled' areas, some practitioners consciously exploiting the boundaries between the two. Whilst preserving traditional craft processes and materials, a major element is creative originality in the ways these skills are developed, adapted and integrated into the design and making process.

Taxonomy of Value Indicators

So far the notion of 'value' in craft objects has been explored, alongside the 'values' that they embody. To further clarify the former, it is necessary to examine the indicators that contribute to, and define, values; which move the object beyond its immediate functionalism through 'added value'. Vaizey (2007) points out 'But nothing here is functional or useful – though functionality is occasionally aped – which implicitly defies at least one disputed aspect of contemporary craft'. The following taxonomy identifies some major added value indicators:

- **Materials** – precious materials, rare materials, materials associated with nature, materials that require complex or skilful processing, materials that have particular historical and/or cultural traditions

- The positioning of the work within a personal (or group) '**body of work**' – within an exhibition or the long-term artistic development of a known practitioner

- The degree of **'discernable skill'** with which the work is imbued

- The quality of **artistic development and integrity** evident in the work

- The '**uniqueness**' of the work, in comparison with the mass-produced

- Alignment with a regional or **heritage** aspect

- Association with an uncommon set of **making skills**

- The use of uncommon **processes and tools**, 'crafts people have always been good at exploiting and manipulating technologies. They use scaled-down version of tools in industry, and this has always been true' (Aldersey-Williams quoting Martin Woolner, 2007: 37)

- The potential for error associated with **risk-taking**, '"mistakes" that occur in the making process, which often provide you with the best material to develop' (Aldersey-Williams quoting Naomi Filmer, 2007: 37).

Further Debates

The paper has explored the interplay of 'financial value' and 'human values' unique in contemporary crafts, attempting to define some of the complex factors that contribute to this interplay. In suggesting that the market for contemporary crafts is less successful than it might be, a number of supplementary issues are raised for further debate; these include: discussion of the ways conscious manipulation of values might be better promoted, understood and exploited; how processes and values might be more effectively communicated to increase value and hence make the contemporary crafts more sustainable via a wider audience of informed and enthusiastic consumers (Aldersey-Williams quoting Luke Prowse of Neville Brody's Research Studios, 2007: 39: 'Showing the process as well as the end product people gain a sense of the dialogue'); to investigate how the Internet might be used more effectively for indirect communication of values. With increasingly varied production techniques becoming available crafts now inhabit a wider production spectrum; in previous eras there was a clearer distinction between volume production and handcrafts. A more flexible approach to production, which fuses volume production with uniqueness, might result in a more sustainable craft base which increases financial value without sacrificing unique values that characterise contemporary crafts (see *Table 3*).

PRODUCTION SECTOR	AUTOMATED MASS PRODUCTION	FLEXIBLE MASS PRODUCTION	HAND-FINISHED MASS PRODUCTION	VOLUME HANDMADE	CONTEMPORARY CRAFTS
PRODUCTION METHOD	Early, inflexible manufacturing systems	Flexible manufacturing systems	Mixed mass manufacture and hand production	Developing world production	The crafts
PRODUCT CHARACTERISTICS	Limited choice, ubiquitous commodities	Highly variable, customised products	Upmarket, luxury commodities	'World design', tourist and/or ethnic goods	Personalised, unique, one-offs
MARKET	Mass market	Mass market	Exclusive	Tourism, niches, low-cost	Specialist

Table 3. The positioning of contemporary crafts within the production continuum

Conclusion

Western society is undergoing profound social changes as it shifts from being an industrial to being a post-industrial society, or from a Modernist to PostModernist society, with all this means in terms of such things as the changing role of leisure in relation to work. An emphasis on the quality of life is, for the prosperous inhabitants of the West, replacing an emphasis on quantity. This not only applies to personal ownership in a time of relative abundance but, for example, to technological matters, where the obsession with making a machine which is faster or bigger is being questioned by those who believe that the machine should be more socially and environmentally useful and responsible. (Whiteley, 1993: 160)

The complex 'explicit/implicit values' of contemporary crafts and related 'commercial value' has been discussed in relation to mass-produced commodities. Issues identified for further exploration include: Do crafts need to change, become more cognisant of their covert roles, in order to develop? Is it necessary to 'educate' current /future generations about the qualities imbued in crafts to create, through understanding, a broader appreciative audience/ consumer? As Frayling wrote in 1986 'the complex traditions out of which contemporary craftwork has emerged have been seriously neglected by scholars and critics alike'. Twenty years on there is still a paucity of well researched, strategic writing, much investigative work and analysis remains to be done.

Finally here is a grounded reasoning for craft objects that endure the passage of time:

We need the reassurance of living with objects which are quite clearly the work of one particular identifiable individual person, working in a particular place, on a particular day, and within a particular tradition. We need human objects as part of our own search for identity and wholeness. We need wood and clay and stone and natural fibres speaking directly to us as part of our search to re-establish contact with nature. This is not a cry against progress and change, but an affirmation that to face the ever-accelerating change as we must, we need to be secure and rooted and centred in our own identity, and connected to our human and natural surroundings. (Keating, 1984)

It is possible that the real value of the craft product is that it is a symbol for social and environmental responsibility, striking a balance between creative work and the enjoyment of a fulfilling existence, whilst reducing the dependency of contemporary consumer society on environmentally harmful production processes. I refer to a quotation from Bruce (2001) 'that hand-work really does allow expression of a man's soul and self, and so is worth doing for its own sake, and worth purchasing even at some cost to the buyer'. The time is now appropriate for a more informed and strategic debate to be engendered which supports a conscious articulation and manipulation of value indicators by practitioners, which will improve the societal positioning of contemporary crafts in this new millennium.

Further Reading

Aldersey-Williams, H. (2007) A Perfect Fit? *Crafts*, 204 Jan/Feb 2007. London, Crafts Council, pp 36–41.

Art New Zealand. (2009) *Mile-Posts and Relationships World Ceramics from the Auckland Museum*. [Online] Available from: http://www.art-newzealand.com/Issues1to40/ceramics.htm [Accessed 8th April 2010].

Borjessen, K. (2007) *The Affective Sustainability of Objects; A Search for Causal Connections. Studies of Theory, Processes and Practice Related to Timelessness as a Phenomenon*. London, Central St Martin's College of Art and Design, University of the Arts London. [PhD thesis].

Bruce, I. (2001) *The Loving Hand and Skilful Eye – The Keswick School of Industrial Arts'*. Carlisle, Bookcase.

Crafts Council. (2010) [Online] Available from: http://www.craftscouncil.org.uk [Accessed 18th April 2010].

Craft Scotland. (2010). *Craft Organisations*. [Online] Available from: http://www.craftscotland.org/craftsorgs.html [Accessed 8th March 2010].

Craft Victoria. (2010) [Online] Available from: http://www.craftvic.asn.au/aboutus/CraftVictoriaVenueHire2010.pdf [Accessed 8th March 2010].

Crouch, P. and Barnes, J. (2001) A Brief History of the Keswick School of Industrial Art. [Online] Available from: http://www.allerdale.gov.uk/downloads/page16/Download%20KSIA.pdf. [Accessed March, 2010].

Department for Business, Innovation and Skills (BIS). (2010) [Online] Available from: http://www.bis.gov.uk/ [Accessed 18th April 2010].Dormer, P. (ed.) (1997) *The Culture of Craft*. Manchester, Manchester University Press. pp. 219 and 228.

Emotional Wardrobe. (2006) Aims. [Online] Available from: http://www.emotionalwardrobe.com/aims.htm [Accessed 18th April 2010].

Frayling, C. (1986) Foreword. In: Pye, D. et al. *David Pye: Wood Carver and Turner*. London, Crafts Council, p. 9–11.

Jones, S. (2007a) News: Creative Scotland consultation. *a-n Magazine*, 2, 18.

Jones, S. (2007b) News: Future Arts funding in Wales. *a-n Magazine*, 2, 19.

Jones, S. (2007c) News: Strategic developments. *a-n Magazine*, 2, 20.

Keating, J. (1984) Foreword. In: Shaw-Smith, D. (ed.) *Ireland's Traditional Crafts*. London, Thames & Hudson, p. 7.

Kelley, C. (2001) *The Arts and Crafts Sourcebook*. London, Thames and Hudson.

Levinson S., and Balkin J.M. (1991). *Law, Music, and Other Performing Arts, Part IV*. Originally published in 139 U. Pa. L. Rev. 1597 (1991). Copyright J.M. Balkin and Sanford Levinson.

Loughborough University. (2006) *Honorary Degree Orations*. [Online] Available from: http://www.lboro.ac.uk/service/publicity/degree_days/2006/Summer/Mellor.html [Accessed 8th March 2010].

McDonough, W. and Braungart, M. (2002) *Remaking the Way we Make Things Cradle to Cradle*. New York, North Point Press, p. 51.

Marks and Spencer Group plc. (2010) [Online] Available from: http://www.marksandspencer.com [Accessed 8th March 2010].

Mellor, D. (2010) *Who We Are*. [Online] Available from: http://www.davidmellordesign.com [Accessed 8th March 2010].

Nicol, G. (2007) *Playing up. a-n Collections* [Online] Available from: http://www.a-n.co.uk/artists/publications/shortcut/article/341804 [Accessed 8th April 2010].

Pye, D. (1968) *The Nature and Art of Workmanship*. Cambridge, Cambridge University Press, p. 133.

Pye, D. (1986) In: Pye, D. et al. *David Pye: Wood Carver and Turner*. London, Crafts Council, p. 53.

Scottish Government. (2010) [Online] Available from http://www.scotland.gov.uk/Topics/ArtsCulture [Accessed 18th April 2010].The Secret World of Haute Couture Television programme BBC 2 Documentary: 3rd April 2007 23:20 to 00:20.

Thomas, G. (2007). New ACE Launched. *a-n Magazine*, 2, 4.

Vaizey, M. (2007) Review of Hung, S. and Magliaro, J. (eds.) By Hand: the use of craft in contemporary art, Princeton Architectural Press, 2006. In *Crafts*, 204 Jan/Feb 2007. London, Crafts Council.

Whiteley, N. (1993) *Design for Society*. New York, Reaktion Books Ltd. p. 160.

Resources

Organisations

Arts and Humanities Research Council
Whitefriars
Lewins Mead
Bristol
BS1 2AE
+44 (0) 117 987 6500
enquiries@ahrc.ac.uk
www.ahrc.ac.uk

Crafts Council
44a Pentonville Road
Islington
London
N1 9BY
+44 (0) 207 806 2500
info@craftscouncil.org.uk
www.craftscouncil.org.uk

Crafts Council of Ireland
Castle Yard
Kilkenny
Ireland
+353 (0) 56 7761804
info@ccoi.ie
www.ccoi.ie

Craft Northern Ireland
Cotton Court
42, Waring Street
Belfast
BT1 2ED
+44 (0) 28 9032 3059
info@craftni.org
www.craftni.org

Jerwood Foundation
22 Fitzroy Square
London, UK
W1T 6EN
+ 44 (0) 20 7388 6287
jerwood@jerwood.org
www.jerwood.org

Scottish Arts Council
12 Manor Place
Edinburgh, UK
EH3 7DD
+44 (0) 131 226 6051
help.desk@scottisharts.org.uk
www.scottisharts.org.uk

World Craft Council
Auras Corporate Centre, Third Floor
98-A Dr. Radhakrishnan Salai
Chennai 600 004 India
+91.44.28478500
wcc.sect.in@gmail.com
www.worldcraftscouncil.org

Places to Visit

Black Mountain College
56 Broadway
Asheville, NC
28801
+1 828 350 8484
bmcmac@bellsouth.net
www.blackmountaincollege.org

Cardiff Castle
Castle Street
Cardiff
CF10 3RB
Wales
United Kingdom
 +44 (0) 29 2087 8100
cardiffcastle@cardiff.gov.uk
www.cardiffcastle.com

Charleston House
The Charleston Trust
Charleston Firle
Lewes
East Sussex, UK
BN8 6LL
info@charleston.org.uk
+44 (0) 1323 811265
www.charleston.org.uk

Craft Study Centre – Museum of Modern Crafts
Crafts Study Centre
University for the Creative Arts
Falkner Road
Farnham
Surrey, UK
GU9 7DS
+44 (0)1252 891450
craftscentre@ucreative.ac.uk
www.csc.ucreative.ac.uk/index.cfm?articleid=3899

Crystal
Hudiksvallsgatan 4B
113 30 Stockholm
Sweden
info@crystalcontemporaryart.se
+46 (0)8 322850
www.crystalpalace.se

Falkland Palace
Falkland
Cupar
Fife, UK
KY15 7BU
+44 (0) 844 4932186
www.nts.org.uk/Property/93

Places to Visit

Gustavsbergs Konsthall
+46 (0)8 570 132 99
info@gustavsbergskonsthall.se
www.gustavsbergskonsthall.se

Mansfield Traquair Centre
+44 (0) 131 555 8475
enquiries@heritageportfolio.co.uk
www.mansfieldtraquair.org.uk/

Mount Stuart
Isle of Bute, UK
PA20 9LR
+44 (0)1700 503877
contactus@mountstuart.com
www.mountstuart.com

National Gallery of Scotland
The Mound
Edinburgh, UK
EH2 2EL
+44 (0)131 624 6200
nginfo@nationalgalleries.org
http://www.nationalgalleries.org/

National Museums Scotland
Chambers Street
Edinburgh, UK
EH1 1JF
www.nms.ac.uk/

Portmeirion Village
http://www.portmeirion-village.com
+44 (0)1766 770 000

Victoria and Albert Museum
V&A South Kensington
Cromwell Road
London, UK
SW7 2RL
+44 (0)20 7942 2000
vanda@vam.ac.uk
www.vam.ac.uk

Online Resources

Art Value
A research project on trash and
readymades, arty and ceramics
Jorunn Veiteberg
Bergen National Academy of the Arts
Stroemgt. 1
N-5015 Bergen
Norway
jorunn.veiteberg@khib.no
www.k-verdi.no

Attainable Utopias
Goldsmiths
University of London
Department of Design
Room 305
The Lockwood Building
Goldsmiths College
University of London
London, UK
SE14 6NW
+44 (0)20 7919 7788
info@attainable-utopias.org
http://attainable-utopias.org/tiki/AuVision

Autonomatic
3D Digital Production
Research Design Centre
University College Falmouth
Tremough Penryn
Cornwall, UK
TR10 9EZ
+44 (0)1326 370497
www.autonomatic.org.uk

Craft and the Creative Process
Smithsonian Institute
www.aaa.si.edu/exhibits/pastexhibits/craft/index.htm

Craftivism
betsy@craftivism.com
www.craftivism.com

Crafts Council: Research and Information
www.craftscouncil.org.uk/professional-development/
research-and-information

Craft Research
Knowledge through Making
www.craftresearch.blogspot.com

Designed Objects
http://designedobjects.blogspot.com

Hidden Art
www.hiddenart.com
info@hiddenart.co.uk
+44 (0)20 7729 3800

Open Source Embroidery project
www.open-source-embroidery.org.uk/osembroidery.htm

Past, Present and Future Craft Practice
Duncan of Jordanstone College of Art and Design
University of Dundee
22 Springfield
DD1 4JE
+44 (0) 1382 388966/388861
www.futurecraft.dundee.ac.uk

Recording the Crafts
University of the West of England
School of Creative Arts
Bower Ashton Campus
Kennel Lodge Road
Off Clanage Road
Bristol
BS3 2JT
matthew.partington@uwe.ac.uk
www.uwe.ac.uk/sca/research/rtc/index.htm

The Making – Contemporary Art, Craft and Design
Civic Office
London Road
Basingstoke
Hampshire
RG21 4AH
+44 (0) 1256 845 679
admin@themaking.org.uk
www.themaking.org.uk/index.html

Think Tank
A European Initiative for the Applied Arts
info@thinktank04.eu
www.thinktank04.eu

WeWorkInAFragileMaterial
+46 (0) 8 6810173
www.weworkinafragilematerial.com